IN CLOVER

BOOKS BY MYRA SCOVEL
PUBLISHED BY THE WESTMINSTER PRESS

In Clover

The Weight of a Leaf

IN CLOVER

MYRA SCOVEL

𝒲

THE WESTMINSTER PRESS
PHILADELPHIA

First edition
Published by The Westminster Press®
Philadelphia, Pennsylvania

PRINTED IN THE UNITED STATES OF AMERICA
9 8 7 6 5 4 3 2 1

Library of Congress Cataloging in Publication Data

Scovel, Myra.
  In clover.

  1. Scovel, Myra. 2. Scovel, Frederick Gilman.
3. Presbyterians—United States—Biography. 4. Missionaries—Asia—Biography. 5. Retirement—United
States—Biography. I. Title.
BX9225.S355A34   285'.1'0922 [B]   79–24882
ISBN 0–664–21366–9

For F., always
and for J., D., J., and E.
for C., F., H., C., and R.
for A., J., D., A., and L.
for T., J., D., and D.
for J., J., E., and J.
for V., J., M., and L.
and for all who come after

Put on your old grey bonnet
with the blue ribbon on it,
While I hitch old Dobbin to the shay,
And through the fields of clover,
We'll drive up to Dover
on our Golden Wedding day.*

PREFACE

I remember the song about the old grey bonnet with its blue ribbon. It came out when I was four years old and it was still going strong when I was old enough to wonder about the lyrics.

Here was an old couple, *very* old, I thought then —old enough to have been married fifty years! They should have been sitting quietly and sadly in their worn-out, stuffy living room doing nothing, not even talking because it would take too much energy to shout.

Instead, this dear man was saying to his little old wife: "Put on that pretty bonnet of yours. I'll harness the horse and we'll drive into the city and celebrate!"

Perhaps it was the music, but he really sounded as if they were both very much in love. I could picture her with her head against his shoulder as he drove through the summer fields. Was it possible to still be in love when one grew old?

I almost named the book "Through Fields of Clover." Then I remembered that there would be many of its readers who would never have the opportunity of seeing those luckiest of cows contentedly munching the fragrant little lavender-pink flowers, feeling, no doubt, as people do when they say they are IN CLOVER.

M.S.

ONE

Sunday Morning, August 30, 1970

Dearest Children and "Grands,"

Friday was the happiest day of my life. You all know that your father has "come of age" (and then some!) and will soon be retiring from our good old United Presbyterian Commission on Ecumenical Mission and Relations. Just between us, I don't see how it's going to get along without him, especially the overseas medical work in which he has been so closely involved for forty years to the month! And I can't help wondering what *he* is going to do without *it*. But back to my happiest day.

The staff organization gave him a farewell retirement party to end all farewell retirement parties. I drove to New York with him.

"I thought your excuse was a bit flimsy," he said later. But neither of us ever dreamed of anything this special.

We arrived at the Interchurch Center, where someone asked him to help an elderly couple to get to the second bank of elevators on the ninth floor. This was to bring him nearer the reception desk where he was to see a huge poster announcing the affair of the day. Not, mind you, "Farewell Party for Frederick G. Scovel, M.D., F.A.C.P.," as one would expect in such a dignified environment, but a sign in brilliant colors, with hearts and flowers cavorting around the words "Love-in for Fred!"

"Who put that thing up?" he wanted to know. Just then a few of the girls ran up to kiss him or give him a big hug. Around their necks were hung heart-shaped cardboard medallions, also saying "Love-in for Fred." As we went down the corridors, everyone we met was wearing one, including John Coventry Smith himself!

Fred was flabbergasted and, as you would know, *very* embarrassed. I couldn't help wondering what the founding fathers and mothers of The Presbyterian Board of Foreign Missions would say if they could have seen their offices Friday. Diane, Fred's secretary, Gertrude Nyce of the executive staff, whom some of you remember from India, and many others must have spent days preparing all of this, busy as they are with their own heavy commitments.

On Fred's desk were piles of cards and gifts. People were running in off and on all morning. In the afternoon we were given a scrumptious tea—all kinds of goodies and a delicious punch (unspiked, in case you are worried!). The table had a huge bouquet of red and white carnations, which we were given. I was also presented with a corsage of pink roses. They looked lovely on my aqua dress.

Gertrude was mistress of ceremonies. She made a flattering speech about our arrival in India when she first met us. Then, from all over the Leber Room, people began speaking; the first two prompting the rest, saying, "I love Fred because . . ." How I wish you could have heard the tributes that were given to your father! When Gertrude asked, "Anyone else?" I couldn't resist saying, "I love Fred and I love every one of you for making this such a beautiful day for him."

But the party was not over. Don Smith arose and surprised us both by reading excerpts from my book, *The Chinese Ginger Jars,* choosing the portions about Fred's being shot during the Sino-Japanese War. I'll set them down here, so if any of you want to save this letter for the grandchildren, you'll have it all here in one place:

A drunken Japanese soldier had come into the hospital courtyard waving a gun and looking for nurses. (The gun wasn't loaded, but nobody knew that then.) Fred and some of his staff were on the grounds and two of the men took the gun away from the man. Another went to the street entrance to find a Japanese guard who would take the drunken one away. But the guard, either misunderstanding the situation or interpreting it as a slur on the Japanese Army, drew out his own gun and forced the men to return the weapon to the troublemaker. By this time the soldier was furious. He put a clip of five bullets in the gun, singled out Fred and motioned him to lead the way to the nurses' quarters. Fred stepped into the path, thinking to lead the soldier back to the guard. The rest of the group scattered.

Fred was about fifteen feet ahead when the soldier shot him through the back. A second bullet went wide of its mark because Fred had fallen. As he lay there, the soldier came and stood over him, with three bullets left in his gun. He aimed at Fred's head and pulled the trigger. Drunk though he was, he could not miss, but the gun did not go off. (People who know these guns tell us they never jam

—not even when hot after having been fired all day.) Again the soldier tried, and again. Finally he wandered off into the street.

After some moments, Fred was able to get up and walk into the hospital. It was typical of him that, with two first-class rooms empty, he put himself to bed in the large third-class ward.

Later, at home, the Japanese General asked if Fred wanted the man who had wounded him shot.

"No, by all means, no," said Fred vehemently. "What good would that do? He was so drunk he didn't know what he was doing. He has nothing against me personally. I feel sorry for the poor fellow. I hear he's been sick and was left behind by his regiment. He has nothing to do all day except to get drunk and make trouble."

There was further conversation about better discipline of the troops in the city.

"It shall be as you wish, Doctor," said the General. "You speak of having climbed Mount Fujiyama. I came here expecting to find an enemy and I find a man whose heart is as kind as Fujiyama is high."

The church was opened the morning after Fred was shot, though it was a weekday. More than a thousand Chinese friends knelt to give thanks to God for saving their doctor's life. I could not leave him to attend the service, but Deane Walter wrote us of how the pastor had taken this opportunity to tell again the story of Christ's coming to earth and giving His life for us all. "So God uses even the wrath of man to praise Him," the letter ended.

We talked about it as Fred lay there, how you work so hard on the mission field, year after year, with no apparent results. Then suddenly one day, doing just the next thing that has to be done, something is accomplished, some wall broken down—not by your planning at all, but by the very circumstances of the hour.

As the reading ended, handkerchiefs were appearing all over the room. I hadn't realized before how much of Fred's character and his witness are portrayed in those few paragraphs. He was, of course, embarrassed beyond words. But he took it like a man and made a very good, short, thank-you speech.

So, dear children, your father is officially retired.

Big hugs all around,
Mom

TWO

I first saw him in the corridor of the Cortland County Hospital in New York State.

"Don't give your heart away until you have met Frederick Scovel," said the director of nurses soon after I had taken the post of supervisor of obstetrics.

"Who is Frederick Scovel?" I asked, trying to appear enthusiastic.

"He's the son of the Presbyterian minister—a medical student who'll be working in the lab for the summer."

"Oh?"

Interest quickened when I saw the full six feet, two and a half inches of him walking down the hall—brown eyes, brown hair, his face very much alive as he talked to our chief surgeon. Not bad at all! But he hadn't even noticed the shrimp of a brunette a foot and a half inch shorter than he. When we did look at each other, we fell in love. (I love the sound of the vowels and consonants in those beautiful words.) In no time at all, we were within that circle of light and warmth, feeling more and more assured that we had found what we had always hoped to find—God's perfect choice for each of us. Never in fifty years have we had occasion to question it. We were married the day after Fred graduated from Cornell Medical College, June 15, 1929.

In September of the following year, we arrived in Peking; with us, our four-month-old son. There we spent a year studying the language and culture of China. It was just the preparation we needed for our almost thirty years in that country and later in India.

Our first hospital was a row of mud huts in the interior of Shantung Province. Later, a school building was converted to what seemed to us then a very modern facility. I taught some of the nursing courses. Along with having four more babies, I also taught our children through eighth grade. We survived six years of the Sino-Japanese War, most of it within the sound of gunfire; some of it within range. Then we were taken to a Japanese internment camp, where we were held for six months, returning to America on the Swedish rescue ship, the *Gripsholm.* We made it just in time (and only *just*) for the birth of our sixth child. I had wanted seven boys and Fred had wanted girls, so we had three of each.

"They call it family planning," Fred would say.

The year 1946 found us in Huai Yuan, Anhwei Province, where Fred's job was to rehabilitate a hospital partly destroyed during the fighting. Peace was short-lived. As the Communists came down from the north, we moved ahead of them to Canton, where Fred was needed for teaching Chinese doctors in the medical college.

Our beloved Father Scovel had died in 1932 and Mother Scovel was living with us. The blessing of having a live-in grandmother is one few missionary children have, and our children fully appreciated theirs.

But her Parkinson's disease had been getting worse and on December 2, 1948, she went on to the place prepared for her.

The following October, the Communists caught up with us. We could be thankful to God that she was spared the difficulties, especially our weeks of being under house arrest.

January 24, 1951! Who could forget that hallowed day when, at last, we were allowed to cross the border from Canton into freedom in Hong Kong! And how can one describe the joy of our return to our home country, much as we would miss our dear, loyal Chinese friends. Some of them had put themselves in dangerous positions by continuing to help us, in spite of our begging them not to take such risks.

In Stony Point, Rockland County, New York, we were free of the onus of putting friends in such a position, free to speak our thoughts without endangering ourselves or our children, free to live in a country where justice and truth were part of the pattern of living. How little we had appreciated all this before; and how much we had taken for granted! But we could revel in it now, and we did for two wonderful years.

Then Fred received a request from our mission board to serve for six years at the Christian Medical College, Ludhiana, in the Punjab of North India. He is a teacher to his fingertips and had been heartbroken when the Communists made it impossible for him to continue his teaching in Canton. Part of his reason for his deciding to take the Canton call had been the earlier urging of our friend, a Chinese magistrate.

"Don't stay on in a small hospital," he had said. "When you die, the work will die with you. Get out and do something big for China; teach and train Chinese doctors to carry on after you've gone. Remember our proverb, 'If I can help a hundred, shall I be content with ten? If I can help a thousand, shall I stop at a hundred?' "

Now Fred was being given the opportunity to do this "something big" in India. He would be professor of medicine, part of an enlarged staff which was to upgrade the college to meet government standards for the M.B.B.S. degree, the equivalent of our M.D. (Later, he also became chairman of the Building Committee for a new, modern teaching hospital, along with his other duties.)

It was hard for us to pull up the tender roots so recently transplanted in the soil of our homeland, but it was pure agony to leave the three older children in America for six long, *very* long years. Though the pain of those separations will never be forgotten, we were given the strength to endure it, and God saw each one through his or her difficulties. Perhaps the children are stronger men and women for having had such experiences. I wonder if I could ever bring myself to do it again.

The assignment proved to be an interesting and rewarding one for Fred and the beginning of a new career for me.

First, he bribed me into writing poetry by giving me breakfast in bed any Saturday morning that I would have a poem on his desk by noon. On furlough he had encouraged my taking a Poetry Workshop at Columbia University under the Pulitzer Prize-winning poet Leonora Speyer. Her inspiration and her friendship over the years were a tremendous influence, for which I shall be forever grateful.

Now in India, Fred was urging me to go ahead with

a book of prose about our life in China. As soon as this became known, the United Church of Northern India gave me writing assignments, sharing its experiences with churches in other countries. So began a life of which I might never have dreamed, if it hadn't been for a husband who knew me better than I knew myself and who cared enough to widen my horizon.

We were preparing for our furlough from India in 1959, wondering about our future, praying for God's guidance. The college was expecting our return, but both of us had become more certain each day that we could never again be so far away from our children for such a long period of time. Too, there was a qualified Indian doctor on the staff whom Fred felt strongly should take his place as professor of medicine. As long as Fred stayed on, it was doubtful that this would occur.

Suddenly, as so often happens to a missionary, the whole pattern of our life was changed. We received a letter asking Fred to return to the United States to serve as Secretary of the Christian Medical Council for Overseas Work for the National Council of Churches. (Later he was made associate director of medical mission work for the United Presbyterian Commission on Ecumenical Mission and Relations.)

Stranger yet, I was being asked to take a writing job in the medical department (later, with communications) for the same commission in the same building, 475 Riverside Drive. We could live in Stony Point and commute to New York City. With three children needing college educations, the timing of these invitations was too perfect to have been anything but God's planning for all our lives.

And now, almost a dozen years had passed and we were (and are still) in Stony Point in our beautiful little home overlooking the Hudson River; Fred, just retired after forty years of service. After such a busy, dangerous, joy-filled, hectic, fascinating life, what would retirement be like for him? I had found out two and a half years earlier.

THREE

People ask if we would like to go back to India, to China. Neither Fred nor I have ever wanted to go back—not to the days when we first fell in love (our love is so much richer now); not to India's glorious mountains, fragrant, flowering trees, and beautiful people, though we miss them very much; not to the beloved friends and never-to-be-forgotten memories of the wisdom, humor, warmth, and the culture of China and its people.

We were in China far longer than we were in India. The thousands of years of the Chinese learning how to respect one another, how to live with one another, have produced a culture that has given us and our children much for which we are grateful. For instance, the most important person in the family is its oldest member. When a teacher enters the classroom, the students immediately rise to their feet. From early childhood, a child is taught to respect his or her parents. If this sounds stodgy, know too, that a group rarely gets together without a flow of humorous stories, puns, conundrums, and so forth. When friends gather and in the home, there is plenty of laughter.

We find that our years there have left their mark on us. The big things may not show, but little things keep popping up. I shock easily, as the Chinese do, when women reveal parts of their bodies that should remain covered. I take off my glasses when I speak to one to whom I should show respect, and always when I pray, to signify that there is nothing between speaker and listener.

Words of the Chinese language fall into our conversations without our realizing it, or because a certain expression in Chinese fits the meaning better.

I never leave even one kernel of rice in the pan, though I smile remembering that "each one left means a pockmark on your face someday." No, I haven't come to believe the old saying, but after one has seen and known hunger, one does not waste. Even after all we went through, we can appreciate and be grateful for the good the Communists have done in reducing poverty and hunger.

It seems hard for some to realize that the Communists are not a separate race of people. Some were friends before they became Communists; others would have become friends if that had been allowed. A few of the most ardent Communists helped us when we needed it most.

And it isn't that Fred and I close the door on the past. The daily memories of both countries will forbid that ever happening. It's just that the present is too filled with interesting commitments and that the ever-shortening years ahead are too well stocked with all we have yet to enjoy and to accomplish.

Still, who knows where tomorrow may find us? Our lives are in His hands; we live from day to day.

I often wonder what my life would have been like if I had been a woman of this generation. I think back to our third date.

Fred was looking at me as if he were amused about something.

"What's funny?" I asked.

"I was just wondering what that other guy is going to say when he hears I'm going to marry you."

My chin must have dropped to my chest. The nerve of him!

"I shouldn't have said that," he hastened to tell me. "I can't ask anyone to share my life. I'm going to be a missionary."

I couldn't have been more astounded. Already I'd been having a few daydreams, looking at the beautiful homes on Cortland's tree-lined streets, thinking of where he was going to practice, wondering if he might like to have me help in the office. But by no stretch of the imagination could I picture myself as a missionary with long skirts, a sun helmet, and a Bible under my arm. Oh, well, he'd probably change his mind.

I had a lot to learn. We often laugh at his scruples about my sharing life with him. He never proposed (neither did I) and I never said I would marry him until we made our vows before his father in the First Presbyterian Church. To us it seems as if it all just happened, inevitably.

It was Mother Scovel who told me that Fred had known he was going to be a medical missionary before he knew that "medical" meant being a doctor. Yet his parents could not remember, nor can he, any person who might have thus influenced him. The longer I knew him, the more I realized that for him God's call had to come first, no matter what sacrifice he might have to make as a result.

My adjustment to the idea was not easy. Fred's parents must have realized it, but they appeared to take it for granted that I, too, wanted to go to China. Their attitude helped a lot because I did not have to be on the defensive. They were helpful in other ways; conversations that came up spontaneously introduced me to their friends who were missionaries in other countries and in our own. They got out books by a missionary to Africa, Jean Kenyon Mackenzie (a book about her is in process), which were just what I needed. Jean was a fascinating writer with a delightful Scot's sense of humor. I began to see that missionaries were very normal people, that there were even published writers among them. The reason I had chosen nursing as a profession was that it was the only education we could afford. But I loved it and it was the ideal preparation for the life I had never expected.

For one thing, I had been taught to meet emergencies. As a nurse, one sees people as they are, with all their defenses down, and one is given the privilege of doing something about their situation. There is no time for the wringing of hands or for "going to pieces." I know of no other profession where one can learn more about people.

As the days of our preparation went by, I began to feel an assurance that since He had led me in this direction and given me training for it, this must be what He wanted me to do, and therefore I could trust Him to be with me the rest of the way. It might be an interesting challenge to see if I could make a home for us wherever and however we lived.

My dear father found it heartbreaking even to think

of my going. Mother realized that a woman had to go where her husband's work was. It never occurred to me to think otherwise.

In a way, it was easier for us in those days. Life patterns were firmly set. It was not a heroic thing that I was doing but the accepted thing. That life patterns for women needed changing came home to me clearly when I went to work in New York and saw women taking second place in the office hierarchy for a third-place salary while carrying first-place knowledge and work load. If first place became empty, it was not the qualified second-place load bearer who took over, but a male, often with no experience whatever, who had to be taught his job by the load bearer along with her usual responsibilities, with no thought of time and a half for overtime. This would not happen today.

In marriage, there is still another side of the question. One does not have to be in that state long before one realizes that it is more blessed (a happier thing) to give than to receive. In fact, it is *only* in giving all of oneself fully to the other, with no strings attached, that one gets. Supposing I had said to Fred: "I have a good job which I am not willing to give up. You can build a practice here in Cortland. I'll help you all I can."

More than likely, he would have broken our engagement, however painful it might have been to him. But supposing he had been willing to go against what he knew was the right thing to do. He would only have been half of what he might have been. Both of us would have been shouldered with a guilt complex.

When I remember that at one time Fred was the only fully trained doctor in an area of five million people, and compare what he did there with what he would have done in competition with five or six other doctors in the Cortland area, I shudder at the thought.

And how much our children would have missed in friendships across the world, in a knowledge and understanding of people of other cultures, of the fun of mountain-climbing in the Himalayas, in choosing a certain husband or wife, in finding a lifework!

And how much I would have missed by staying on at the Cortland County Hospital, much as I love that town and its people! I wonder if I would ever have taken pen in hand. Now I cannot imagine life without it.

It isn't a question of "me first," or "he first"; it is God first. It is a question of two persons who are so much in love that each wants the other to lead a happy life, fulfilled in every way. It is knowing that the only way to be sure of this is for them to seek God's will together; to wait until it becomes clear to both what path they are to take—even if one or the other has a few qualms about what he or she may meet on the way. If one is sure of God's will, there is no need for fear or reservations. He can be trusted to see one through.

In any marriage, there are times of disappointment and misunderstanding. We all prefer to have our own way, and we know there are times when we must give in. I once came across part of a sentence which I found written on the inside back cover of an old Bible. It read: ". . . that old myth, so hard to dispel, that personal happiness is important."

The words of my mother came back to me: "Never go halfway. Don't say to yourself, 'If he comes halfway, I'll meet him there.' He won't. Go the whole way and he will too."

What *is* important, and what brings with it real happiness, is that with God, it is never too late for a new beginning.

In the summer of 1967, we had a new beginning to consider, a change I almost feared to make.

FOUR

Fred gave me an electric typewriter for my sixty-second birthday. We had begun to talk about my early retirement. We wondered how much longer I could continue to get up at five, work an hour on the current book, leave at seven for a full day's work at the office, arrive home at six to get dinner, do the washing, and so on. Fred helped all I would let him, but he usually came home with a full briefcase and rarely got to bed before twelve. He insisted upon doing the supper dishes. Fortunately, a dear friend came in once a week to do the heavy cleaning. Without her, I do not think I could have continued to write.

In spite of the good help I had, my diary is filled with such entries as:

> I am tired of never being anything—wife or mother or friend. I do nothing but work. *Current News* is a week late; the book isn't finished; and the stack of mail not touched.

That particular entry was followed by this one:

A lovely Saturday. Fred won't let me speak or even think about work. He brought me breakfast in bed, a brown-gold pansy on the tray, his dear love around me. Who could want more?

Why, with all I had, was I so frustrated? Because I was overtired? self-centered? Should I give up writing? I'd be more frustrated than ever, but perhaps I could learn to rise above it. I certainly was not easy to live with, and Fred did not deserve *that*. What about that verse from Isaiah? "Why do you spend money and get what is not bread? And your labor and go unsatisfied?" And my oft-quoted line from the Westminster Catechism? "The chief end of man is to glorify God and enjoy him forever." When was I going to begin to *enjoy* him? I was spending all my time griping.

Somewhere I had run across the sentence, "Wholeness comes with the rooting out of incompatibles." It reminded me of India, where it was customary for men of culture to retire at the age of sixty for a few years or for the rest of their lives. They would leave their families and go off to some holy place where they could meditate. It was a time to zero-in on essentials.

"Man has to choose between knowing a small bit about a lot, or settling down to what he wants to do with the rest of his life," said an Indian friend of ours, a businessman.

We had spent so many years of our life living in the future. Will our money last until the end of the month? We'll do this or that when the children grow up, when the war is over, when we retire, when I have time. How much time did I have? Imagination can run wild. What if this were my last day alive? What if there were no life after death? What if the only life I would ever have with those I loved was right here, now? What if the only relationship I was going to have with God was right here, now?

"You really don't believe any of this," I said to myself.

"Yes, but *what if?*"

If I could do anything I wanted to do, what would be my first priority?

I'd live in a place that was nearest to my idea of heaven. Well, that was right here, now . . . when I had time to be here! Nothing could be more like heaven than writing all day, with breaks for setting things right in the house—dusting the old furniture that had been in Fred's family for generations, freshening up the curtains, arranging the flowers, doing all the things I now looked at as I ran past and cringed that they were not being done. Cooking was an ideal change from desk work, not just slapping food together, but cooking! A good-sized washing wasn't bad either, especially if the clothes could be hung in the sun. It was beginning to look as if some of the incompatibles would have to go. And the incompatibles were not to be found at home. How did I dare to take such a step? This was going to take time, thought, and prayer.

Was it fair to leave the whole financial burden on Fred's shoulders? What I had made on my books had gone into the children's educations, and how grateful we were that we had the money then! What if this next book wasn't accepted by the publishers? At best, the royalties wouldn't keep us alive very long. What if there were no next book?

Fred couldn't see any reason why I shouldn't retire at once. "You'll be getting your Social Security," he said, "and though the amount is less than it would be if you worked three years longer, it isn't *that* much less.

The kids are either self-supporting or have husbands to look after them. The mortgage is paid. Thank the good Lord we never charge anything, so there aren't any bills hanging over our heads."

"And we aren't people who have to have a new this or that just because a new model comes out," I added.

"So I don't see why you shouldn't retire any day now."

"Fred, you're the most wonderful husband in the world. To think of having the whole day to work on the book! I love you, I love you, I love you! But are you sure we can make it financially? I'd miss commuting with you. What would they say at the office?"

"How long have I been telling you that nobody but you can write what you have to write? Others can do *Current News of the Church Overseas.*"

"And do it better than I."

"I'm not so sure of that," said Fred.

Only a warm, loving, understanding met me at the office, after the arguments against my leaving had been fully expressed.

I looked around at everything those last days at "475," seeing more clearly the strong friendships, the hard work, the thrill of good results, the frustrations, even the mistakes. As one of the girls added, "like setting up the budget and holding it up to God for his approval; yet, he working through us and in us and in spite of us to accomplish his purposes."

I was proud and humbly grateful to have been a part of it.

Another experience awaited me in the same building before I could settle down at home. Friendship Press, publisher of my books for children, needed someone to fill in for a few months until the permanent children's editor could arrive. I loved every minute of it. Yet my diary for that last day, January 5, 1968, reads:

> A strange feeling, coming down on the elevator for the last time. But only joy when I walked into the house, my home, my base. It seemed so right.

It was like being touched with a magic wand. I had everything I wanted. Fred had varnished the floor of my study and painted the walls a silver gray—just the right background for the warm red in the Oriental rug Father Scovel had brought back from Constantinople in 1891. Fred said he was getting the room ready in self-defense. He was getting tired of sleeping in my office.

I had been using one corner of our bedroom. Files were in the clothes closet and down in the basement. I must admit that because of my continued accumulations, it was getting a bit difficult to get in and out of bed. Now we had taken over one of the girls' vacated rooms where there was plenty of space for my desk, writing and typewriter tables, the comfortable overstuffed chair with no arms, where I could compose with pen and pad. Room, too, for the files, a good-sized bookcase and three smaller ones, actually the packing boxes, freshly painted white, in which our books had traveled over the years and now looked comfortably at home.

This was the study I had dreamed of. The question was, Could I write in it? It would take discipline to keep my eyes from the wide windows. The view of the Hudson River and its interesting commerce and the Westchester hills beyond could be seen from anywhere in the room, fascinating in every change of the weather. I had read of writers who had written under the stress of uncomfortable, cramped quarters and who, when given the ideal environment, found the Muse had fled.

I managed to keep my eyes on the paper by setting a rigid time schedule and sticking to it. Once I became involved in what I was writing, it was not difficult and the hours from 9 A.M. to 3:30 P.M., with time out for lunch, sped by like a teen-ager's night out.

By late afternoon, I began to miss Fred. The house felt so empty—no children coming home from school, no sounds except the ones I made. Sometimes it seemed that six o'clock would never come. We weren't used to watching much television, after our many years in the Far East without it, but I discovered *The Mike Douglas Show* which helped a lot.

And I found I could write in ideal surroundings. There were the usual frustrations, of course. The telephone. Take the phone off the hook? People are more important than paper. Yet a ten-minute conversation could take me an hour to pick up my momentum, remember the steps in getting a character out of difficulty, and so forth. I learned to jot down notes in the margin ahead as ideas came, so that I'd remember when I got there. But holding the character alive in one's mind, almost becoming that character throughout an entire situation, could be completely shattered by the ringing of the phone or doorbell. People are more important than paper. But the book was for *people.* I tried to remember that the interruptions just might come from God.

I couldn't complain. In spite of interruptions, a book for Harper & Row, another begun, two books and a one-act play for Friendship Press were published between my retirement and Fred's. Soon we would be together, perhaps for the rest of our lives. A spurt of joy shot through me every time I thought of it. Still, there were misgivings.

FIVE

My mother used to say, "I could never marry a minister, because I couldn't stand having him around the house all the time."

I remember thinking, If I loved a man as much as she loves my father, I'd *want* him around the house all the time.

Now, I wondered. What would this do to my writing schedule? The week before, he had been home with a cold and fever. Not that he wasn't "perfectly able to work." He is always "perfectly able to work." It's just that his "nose is dripping" and he "doesn't want to pass the virus around."

We slept late, had a leisurely breakfast, and he settled down to his reading. I had already lost an hour at my desk. It was wonderful having him home, breakfast without the rush of getting him off to work, but frustration was leaking in around the edges. I decided to forget the book and tackle the pile of unanswered mail.

Voice from downstairs: "I didn't know he wrote that."

I tried to ignore it, but curiosity won the battle. "Wrote what?"

" 'Now is the winter of our discontent . . .' It's from *King Richard the Third,* Act One, Scene One, line one. 'Now is the winter of our discontent made glorious summer by this sun of York.' "

One of my first delights in knowing Fred was seeing how literary quotations popped up in unexpected places. Pay any man a compliment and he will reply, "Gee, thanks!" Fred is far more apt to come out with: "Our praises are our wages. With one soft kiss we ride a thousand furlongs, ere with spur we heat an acre."

Drive into Haverstraw any busy Saturday. Two drivers, going in opposite directions, will have stopped in the middle of the main street, passing the time of day. Most men, waiting to pass, will fume, then shout a few suggestions. Not Fred. Amused, he quotes the Bible: "It was, in Haverstraw, as it was in the days of the Judges, when 'every man did what was right in his own eyes.' "

And now Shakespeare. "What in the world are you doing with *Richard the Third?*" I wanted to know.

"Reading it. What else?"

I had often thought of the *winter* of my discontents without recalling that it "was made glorious summer" by the presence of someone. It was time to remember that we were both getting older and that every day together, every hour, was precious.

During lunch, Fred said: "When I retire I want you to go on with your daily schedule as you usually do. You don't have to retire from your work just because I do."

"We'll take care of that when the time comes," I told him.

I had been keeping my ears open about this retirement business. One dear friend had been active in good works all her life. She had had no thought of dropping out of things when her husband retired. Now she found that he had expected her to retire, too, so they could play golf every day, go on errands together, and so forth. Leisure for her was much more enjoyable if she could also continue with her commitments, which did not take all of her time by any means. Still, her husband felt neglected whenever she went out to a meeting.

On the other hand, my sister and her husband were having the time of their lives. Each of them retired from jobs that had been strenuous physically and that required taking a great deal of responsibility for, and accountability to, others. Now they were both enjoying two rounds of golf in the morning, having lunch, and playing another round in the afternoon. In the winter, they would bowl. After raising eight children, they were alone in the house, happy, and younger than they'd been in years. It was a joy to think of them after the horrendous tales I had heard in the beauty parlor:

"There he sits, taking up the whole corner of the living room, all his newspapers and stuff spread out around him. And will he move when I want to clean? You bet he won't. He can't understand why I clean anyway. I have to wait till he goes out for the paper before I can run the vacuum cleaner. Then he complains he can't find anything."

"I took a week of that and went out and got myself a job," said one lady, looking up from her magazine.

"I wish a friend of mine would do likewise," came a voice from under the dryer. "Her husband sits around all the time, too. And what's worse, he doesn't have much of a pension and she has nothing, not even Social Security. She has to ask him for every cent and explain what she is going to do with it. If it's anything he considers useless, like talcum power or peanuts, she doesn't even bother to ask—just goes without it."

The failure of *that* retirement began with courtship, I thought. For that matter, the success or failure of any retirement, any marriage, begins there. Choosing a life partner can make or ruin a human being, perhaps two human beings. However, a happy marriage is not made so by one of the two acquiescing in everything the other one wants. Two individual personalities are involved, each with separate and often differing ideas, yet opposites often attract and are compatible.

We both consider ourselves the most fortunate, blessed persons on earth to have found each other. I know a lot of prayer went into both our lives as we were growing up. I know, too, that we both knew the *kind* of a person we wanted to marry and would not have married until we found that person, or at least we don't think we would have. Whatever the reasons, we can only be very humbly grateful that it happened to us. We both like to do the same things and we do have some sort of extrasensory perception flowing from one to the other. Long ago we stopped being amazed to find one of us answering a question the other had not yet asked. We get in the car and one says, "Where do you want to go?" More often than not, the answer is the very place the other had in mind.

I told this to one of our friends and she said: "Ah, yes, Myra, I know what happens. One of you, probably Fred, gives in to the other all the time. It saves an argument."

Nobody in our family tries to save an argument. We agree; we also disagree. And we argue; do we ever argue! We disagree on big issues and on little ones; usually on things that don't amount to very much. We express ourselves freely, though never at length. We made it a rule of our lives that we would never, never, never go to sleep without making up. Usually, whatever the argument, it is over in a relatively short time these days. Now we argue without realizing that it is an argument.

Just the other day we started off on something. (Honestly, I don't remember what it was.) I suddenly noticed the face of a neighbor who had dropped in. Her expression was one of excruciating pain, as if she thought the end of our marriage was taking place before her very eyes.

Immediately, I said, "Honey, how about picking a couple of your roses for Mary?"

"Great idea," he replied. "Would you like pink, or yellow, or red, Mary?"

Our daughter Judy explained us very well to a friend she had brought home from college. Embarrassed by our conversation, she said, "My parents argue, but it has nothing to do with their love for each other."

We were both amazed—we are *always* amazed when people think we are arguing. To us it is talking about something we disagree on.

A close friend recently shared with me William Barclay's idea that it is not lack of disagreement that makes marriage good, but that even at the height of contention there is no one else on earth with whom one would rather be at that moment.

Marriage is a blending of personalities that the giving of one's self to the other brings. Unless both are willing to give fully, the marriage is bound to be warped. This is why it is hard for us to see how living together without marriage would help in knowing whether or not it would work, since there is no commitment made by either person.

I heard recently of a young couple who had been living together for six years. It appeared that they had everything going for them. But one evening the man came home and told the girl that he could see that the arrangement would never work for him. He was marrying so-and-so on Saturday.

The sadness of the situation haunts me. Imagine living with someone for six years without ever having had the warmth of *belonging* to each other.

Alas, there are bound to be potholes along the road to the best of marriages, sometimes even craters. I remember very well our early years in China. Fred was overwhelmed with his work at the hospital—some two hundred patients a day in the clinic, to say nothing of the bed patients, operations, a flood of the Yellow River and its victims, a visit of the governor of the province, etc. And his wife complaining, crying because he didn't give her and their children more time.

I should have known better. I should have known that it is physically, mentally, and morally impossible for a doctor to leave suffering people and sit down for an enjoyable evening with his wife and children, especially when he must first listen to a weepy complaint about the little time spent at home.

I *did* know better. But I was nursing my grievances, spending time telling myself what I would say when he got home; how he would reply and what I would say then. I am ashamed to even think of it now.

One day, I came to my senses. Why should he want to come home? He would only get the same harangue over and over again. The children didn't like to hear it either. From now on, I would plan things so that every moment at home would be restful and happy.

He had been gulping down his lunch and hurrying back to the clinic. By choosing his favorite dishes, he became more conscious of what he was eating. Reading a chapter from children's books we all enjoyed together, such as *Mr. Wilmer* or *Mr. Popper's Penguins,* prolonged his stay a few minutes.

In India, we began the habit of having our after-dinner coffee together in the garden, no children allowed. They could talk to him during the meal. This was the only time we two could get caught up on the messages he had received, plans for the present and future, and so forth. Too, he always wanted to tell me about his most interesting cases, about people he had met during the day, the arrival of the first robin, the committee meeting. He still brings me up-to-date on each day's activities that he thinks will interest me.

And he wants to know how far along I am in chapter four; whether or not I have sent out any poems, and if not, why not. When a manuscript is out, his first question on coming home is, "Did you get that letter we're expecting?"

I think he feels more deeply than I do the disappointment of a rejection, and that must be about as deep as it is possible to go. Acceptance calls for a celebration, a gift, roses, dinner at our favorite restaurant.

Nothing is more essential to a happy marriage than for a man and his wife to be able to talk to each other. One of the saddest sentences one can hear from a friend is, "He (or she) wouldn't be interested."

Oh, "young lovers, wherever you are," learn to talk to each other. Tell each other about everything—the little happenings as well as the big ones. Save up interesting things you come across during the day. Pass on the funny things that happen. (We leave magazines on the couch or table, opened at cartoons or good articles.) And never, never let your married life become reduced to a grunt in answer to an empty question.

And as for that poor man in the corner of the living room and his poor wife waiting with the vacuum cleaner, we were making preparations so that we would not run into their difficulties.

Six

We had begun early to make preparations for our old age. For Christmas or birthdays the children gave us or we gave each other reference books on art, poets and their poetry, wild flowers, birds, China, India, Thailand, stamps, coins; late editions of *Roget's Thesaurus, Cruden's Concordance,* the *Columbia Encyclopedia,* and of course dictionaries—two upstairs and two down. We don't even go on a vacation without a dictionary.

Though we are still perfectly capable of running up to the library and do often, we find that during the long winters we are grateful for our reference books. And it certainly saves time, as when I'm in the midst of writing a poem about the Dragon Boat Festival in China and need to check its history while still holding the poem in mind. Our histories of Rockland County came in handy when I was working on a Bicentennial book for our township. And during the collecting of material for a book about poems and poets, including some one hundred and fifty poems, I rarely had to leave the house.

There were other preparations to be undertaken if Fred was to have more than a corner of the living room.

We looked around the house to see where he could be made as comfortable as he had made me. His own study was a very small room opening on the living room. Everything he wanted was within reach. But later, when he would be spending more time there, how could he work on his pastel drawings or practice his two recorders, or spread out his stamps or his Chinese coins or the slides of his wild flower collection?

We decided on the basement room where the children and their families slept when they visited us. There was plenty of light from the three large windows overlooking the river. A board covering one of the single beds would make a table which could be removed easily when the room was used as a bedroom. At most, that would not be more than every month or two since they were all busy people with children in school and the nearest family was some two hours away.

Meanwhile, Fred was making some preparations on his own. His idea of retiring had always been to get a job doing what one is happiest doing "without any administrative work whatsoever." To put it mildly, Fred has never liked administration, though it had been a large part of his life all the years overseas, as well as in New York. He longed to get his hands on patients again and was delighted to be welcomed to the staff as visiting attendant in internal medicine at the New York State Research and Rehabilitation Hospital, just ten minutes from home. (The name has since been changed to Helen Hayes Hospital.) It was a part-time job, three days a week (which soon changed to four and a half). He would begin his duties in November, so we still had time to redo the basement room.

We could hardly wait to tell the good news of Fred's appointment to my brother, Bob, and his wife, Dorothy, at our usual Saturday evening get-together.

"Let's go out to lunch to celebrate soon," I suggested.

"Yes, let's," Dorothy replied. "We'll have to do this more often now that you both will have more time."

"How much longer do you have at the grindstone, Bob?" Fred asked.

"A couple of years, and I wish it were now," said Bob.

"He'll probably be bored stiff," said Dorothy.

"Maybe I will, but right now all I want is to get out of the rat race," said Bob. He took another sip of his milk. (No more coffee until the ulcer healed.) "You have to have a streak of laziness in you to make a success of retirement, and I consider myself highly qualified."

"You haven't a lazy bone in your body," I told him. "You just know how to enjoy leisure. I don't think many people do."

"Let's see, Fred, you've got several weeks before you start work, haven't you?" Bob asked.

"Yes, and I'll be crawling up walls by that time," he replied.

I was shocked to hear it, and so was Dorothy. "You really don't mean that, do you?" she asked.

"We'll just have to wait and see," he replied.

"You'll have a few things to keep him busy, won't you, Myra?" My brother knows me very well.

"That reminds me of what Sara Hazlett calls a 'honeydew' retirement," I replied.

"You mean a honeymoon retirement," said Bob.

"No, 'honeydew.' You know, 'Honey, do this,' and 'Honey, do that!' "

We had a good laugh and many others that evening, but for the first time, I saw that leaving his work in New York and starting out on a new venture was far more difficult for Fred than I had thought—much harder for him than it had been for me. For one thing, I hadn't had to change my environment; my office was at home.

We were painting the basement room one morning. The weather was hot. Fred was perspiring and the smell of paint always bothered him.

"Maybe we'd better stop for a while," he said. He looked as if he might faint. We picked up the folding chairs and took them out to the back lawn.

"Are you sure you're all right?" I asked.

"Sure," he said, rather shakily.

The fresh air helped. The color came back in his cheeks. "We'd better get busy," he said without moving. "When we get this job done, we'll at least have our own separate corners."

"So when we get sparring we'll have them to retire to?" I asked.

"You know better than that," he said.

Did he have a feeling I was shoving him into a corner by putting him off in the basement? He always liked to be in the center of things, and never closed the door to his small room.

No, he didn't think so.

"It's just that I have to get used to things," he said.

I remembered that awful feeling I had had when I first began to write in my new surroundings. Would I be able to work there? I could because my work was a driving force. Fred's driving force had been taken from him when he left his desk in New York. The new job was something he hadn't done in several years. Thoughts of being inadequate in the new situation must have run through his head, for he said, "Medicine moves so fast these days."

"Medicine does, but healing an illness doesn't change much, does it?" I asked.

"No, I suppose it doesn't," he answered.

"Besides, name one doctor that keeps as up-to-date as you do—all those courses you take in New York, the piles of magazines and books you go through . . ."

"Well, we'll see," he replied. "Let's get back to the painting."

We worked quietly for a while; then Fred said, "I sure wish I knew when my pension check would come."

"What do you need it for?" I asked. "To buy a bag of peanuts?"

He didn't even smile, but he realized he had hit on what was really troubling him.

"I guess it's going back to all those years of insecurity we had—when there never was enough money. I've figured things out, as you know, and we should make out all right . . . unless something big happens. And something big can happen any time."

"We should be better off than we've ever been," I reminded him.

It was a strange thing to feel secure when Fred was insecure for the first time I could remember. He had always been the one to say: "Don't worry. God will see us through as he always has in every difficulty."

His own words came back to him and he brightened up at once. From then on, he was the same strong man I had always known.

I did a lot of thinking about this as I saw so many of our friends in the same predicament. Most of them retired with no idea of ever going to work again. Some haven't yet made the adjustment. But my self-styled "lazy" brother was not one of them. He began at once to enjoy life to the full—going off on afternoon expeditions with Dorothy, setting up feeding stations for the birds, delighting in every new species. He became interested in Constitution Island, the Revolutionary War era home of the Warner sisters (who were writers and who had held a popular Sunday afternoon Bible class for the West Point cadets across the river). And of course, he played golf, and still does.

To me, it was very sad to hear him say once that he had seen the tree outside his kitchen door in full bloom for the first time in all the years they had lived there.

"I am not surprised," I told him. "You were always rushing off to work or coming back with your mind full of the bank's problems that were your responsibility to solve."

There is a lot to be said about enjoying life as one goes on working from day to day, *before* it is time to retire. Perhaps one must learn to notice, take time for relaxation. One friend in the office raised miniature plants and brought them in for us to enjoy. Another brought in rare dahlias which he grew. They brightened our workday, and our delight in them increased the pleasure of raising them, I am sure.

Fred had always insisted that for busy people, interesting hobbies are a *must*. Why, then, with the many he had, was leaving the job so upsetting? Especially when he also had a new opportunity to do the very thing he had so much wanted to do.

Perhaps a man's base is his office, his work. Here he is in touch with his world, the people with whom he works and their interests, the latest company policies.

He comes home to rest, to enjoy the family, to drop his anxieties. But he doesn't want to stay there and do only that, all the next day and the next and the next. His coming home is the break in the routine of his working hours. Too, he has the satisfaction of fulfilling his role as man-the-provider. And it is not only man in his office; one could go on and on about the trucker and his truck, the farmer and his farm, the merchant and his store.

Whether or not a woman goes out to work, her base is her home. She may go into the world to break the routine of housework, to help to provide for the family, or she may be its only provider. She comes back to her base to start all over again to catch up on what must be done there. But when the time comes for her to give up working out, she is delighted to be back at her base and able to go where and when she wishes.

Supposing Fred and I had our roles reversed. What if I were going to do my work in his office? I could picture him making a place for me, setting up a desk, moving in a comfortable chair, painting the walls, hanging one of my favorites of his pastels. He would be glad we were going to be together, but he could not help having qualms about how he was going to get his work done. In a way, it would no longer be his office. I would feel out of place, as if I were standing in his way (as Fred was apparently feeling about "being under my feet all the time").

It wasn't a good comparison because he was not butting in, but returning to his own home. The house was every bit as much his as it was mine. I must remember this and never, never for a moment, let him feel that it wasn't. There would be a few changes in my life, but nothing drastic. The anticipation of his evening homecoming would be gone, but that would be exchanged for a leisurely breakfast together. *The Mike Douglas Show*? He just might become interested too. If not, we could take our long walks together, a pleasure we had only on weekends.

We never even tried the basement room. We took a chunk of our savings and enlarged Fred's small study to a size to meet his needs (with the door still opening on the living room). It was worth all we put into it. We were both happy, and with one of us upstairs and the other down, we found we could each concentrate on what we were doing.

Now we were ready to celebrate Fred's retirement by leaving for Mexico and our long-dreamed-of treat of seeing the Ballet Folklórico performed in its home city.

SEVEN

Sunday Again

Dearest Children,

By the time you finish this letter, you will have read all you never wanted to know about Mexico, and more. But we want to share this with you, as we always do, so here goes.

Now that our civilization has reached the "advanced" stage of hijacking, some of our friends thought we were crazy to fly. As you know, there has been a lot of talk about whether or not airports have a right to examine us and our luggage. We were relieved to find that the machines were all set up and that every passenger would be examined.

Our craft was wheeled out to the runways, but was stopped because of another tragedy of which you may have read—the burning of the 727 training plane. As we watched it for almost two hours, the ambulance going and coming, the eleven dead crew members being carried off, our excitement changed to heavy sorrow, but at last we were off, forcing fear and sadness to remain behind. We enjoyed sitting together, reading with no interruptions from phone or doorbell, eating, talking, or just holding hands.

We arrived in Mexico City about 9 P.M. The Hotel Del Prado is in the heart of downtown, but just across from the beautiful Alameda Park. The hotel's claim to fame is a large mural, painted in 1947 by the famous Diego Rivera. It is called "A Dream on a Sunday Afternoon at Alameda Park," and is composed of portraits of people who took part in historical events of their times from Cortez and the Spanish Conquest up to Rivera's time. We'll send you postcards of it. The small boy with the frog and a snake in his pocket is the artist himself.

There had been a great deal of controversy over the sheet of paper in the hands of one of the old patriots. Rivera had inscribed on it, "God does not exist; therefore I cannot swear." People resented this so much that the mural was covered for seven years. One day Rivera walked into the hotel and painted over what he had written, writing instead, "Constitution of 1857."

We were told that the hotel commissioned the work for $6,000. To transfer it to the lobby cost $16,000. But I must get you out into the sunshine.

It is the cleanest city I have ever seen, perhaps because we were fortunate enough to arrive for the celebration of the 160th anniversary of the beginning of their long struggle for independence. The streets were decorated with spectacular lighting; symbols of the struggle were hanging in midair (actually attached to a netting which could not be seen when the lights were on). Streets were crowded with those out to enjoy the sights. Imagine it, with all those people in parks, on the streets, everywhere, there was not one beer can, not a gum wrapper, even in the gutters.

Someone suggested that this could only happen in a

country that still has peons. (The dictionary says, "an unskilled laborer or a farm worker; or one bound in servitude to a landlord creditor.") We couldn't afford to have people constantly picking up after us. Maybe we're caught between the age of the salaried sanitation worker and our failure to use creatively the technology at hand. The museums were immaculate, floors shining like black jade. But in every room, there was a man cleaning the floor all day long with a mop three yards long. (Yes, three yards.)

Of all the museums, our favorite was the National Museum of Anthropology. We began with an orientation movie of a brief history of Mexico. Artifacts from the museum were raised up from the floor below as the lecture went on. This, and a small guidebook, were most helpful.

The exhibits were arranged perfectly, the background colors just the right shade for the item shown, whether it was pottery, jade, wood, or even bones. The gardens which we saw as we went from room to room were part of the exhibit, the garden side being entirely glass with doors leading out. Here were many tombs of ancient kings. At the very moment when I felt I'd had my fill of death, before us in the garden stood an old Mexican farmhouse, every inch of its visible wood hand-carved. And, get this, a live cow was feeding in a manger. The healthy smell of cow, after all the bones and relics, was pure satisfaction. Not that the museum was depressing; many of the clay figures were done by ancient artists adept at mischievous humor.

We had an excellent lunch at the museum restaurant —shrimp salad in a huge avocado, fresh strawberries on ice cream, and coffee. The Mexican salads are mountainous and come on looking like . . . well, *Mexican* salads, brilliant in color and arrangements of red, orange, pink, yellow, and green, just by using their fruits or vegetables.

The outside courtyard around the museum has a roof covering it that looks like a huge umbrella, the "handle" of which is a heavily carved stone column. We were told that this roof was "easily the size of two football fields." To me, the important thing was the torrent of water pouring off the umbrella from all sides, giving off a very cooling spray. I blush to tell you how much time I spent under it (never mind my hairdo or clothes) while Fred was somewhere in the heat looking at every last little statue. You know your father.

We both liked best the statue of the rain god, Tlaloc, which stands at the entrance to the museum, looking down on the people coming and going as if he meant business. (I can't imagine *anyone* sneaking in or out.) They had to build a twenty-wheeled cart to get the 165 tons of him down to the museum, the mountain people protesting to no avail. The story is that as soon as the statue was set in place, there fell upon Mexico City such a downpour as had never before been seen. Fred took a picture of him and I did a crescent verse form about him. For some reason, I have become very fond of that huge, squat, scowling figure. Herewith the poem:

RAIN GOD

Tlaloc,
the torrents fell
when you were set in place
to guard the great museum door.
Were you angry? Your face
I study now—
that look!

And the flowers! The parks were full of them, especially dahlias, the national flower. "Miles of them at

Chapultepec Park," said our hotel hostess. Apparently, everyone gives flowers to everyone else in Mexico. At railway stations, as people arrived or departed, they were being given armfuls of roses. At the flower market, we walked through wooden stalls, marveling at so much beauty in one city block.

We hadn't been in Mexico City more than a couple of days before I began to notice this contrast between the flagrant and the funereal. We saw dark-suited men, and only dark-suited. Even the young girls wore quiet colors and the older women mostly black or gray-blue. But waitresses in restaurants wore colorful costumes, and the food was always arranged with an eye to bright colors. I was pleased to come across these lines from the poem "Discourse on Flowers" by the contemporary poet Carlos Pellicer: "The Mexican people have two obsessions, a liking for death, and a love of flowers."

One of the restaurants we frequented was Sanborn's House of Tiles. It is an old Spanish Colonial building, formerly inhabited by noblemen. The story goes that a certain count told his son, "You'll never have a house of tiles," meaning, "You'll never make it." Well, he *did* make it, and as soon as the house was handed down to him, he covered the whole outside of it with glazed tiles.

We ate in what was once a courtyard where the coaches drove up to the stairway leading to the second floor. Here the family lived. The courtyard has become a huge room with lovely hanging lanterns, but we will remember it because of the couple at the next table.

The gentleman was opening one of those horrid cornucopia things that hold cream for coffee. It splurted straight at me. When I felt the spray across my ankle, I jumped up and found I had cream all over my legs and in my lap. Fred had had such a time with those fool things when we first came back from India that it struck us both funny and we started to laugh, much to the relief of the poor Mexican couple, who were horrified at first.

Well, that is one way to make new friends. They and the waiter soon had me sponged from the waist down. We had a good chat and ran into the couple again at the ballet, where all four of us burst out laughing again.

The Ballet Folklórico was even better than I had dreamed. Oh, what dancing! Not ballet as we know it, but choreographed folk dancing without losing its spontaneity. The idea was conceived and executed by Amalia Hernandez, described by one writer as a woman with "the aethereal grace of a young ballerina and the strategic combat ability of a three-star general." I can't describe the dances, the many changes of costume, nor even give you a glimpse of the pathos and humor portrayed by the dancers. You'll just have to see it, and if at all possible, in Mexico.

The theater itself is fascinating. The Palacio de Bellas Artes is made of such heavy Italian marble that it has sunk into the ground fourteen feet. It seems strange to have to walk down a little hill so you can go up the marble staircase. You will never forget the curtain rising, for it is made of yard-square sections of colored glass, which represent a huge painting of the twin volcanoes that stand guard over Mexico City. By the lighting behind the glass curtain, you see dawn breaking over the snow-capped mountains, the light slowly increasing until it is bright day. By the way, the curtain weighs twenty-two tons and was built by Tiffany of New York about fifty years ago. I'm glad I was not responsible for moving it from New York to Mexico!

The pages are piling up and I haven't told you about our trip to the silversmiths with an off-duty policeman; or to the Museum of Modern Art, where the paintings of Velásquez are on permanent exhibition; or of the guided tour to the pyramids with three vacationing nurses from Texas who really fell for your father. (They were darlings.) They and Fred climbed to the top of the Pyramid of the Sun. I started with them, but my back was serving me notice and I thought I might get a poem if I sat alone in the silence and pondered a civilization so glorious that its *ruins* were protected and, if not revered, at least held in deepest respect. I wondered if we will leave anything but beer cans, and that ugly thought chased away the Muse.

We went to see the Basilica of Guadalupe, where people had come to be healed—a moving experience. You can almost feel the breathing of the Holy Spirit in the deep faith of those around you.

We visited the Carmelite Convent, dating back to 1617. Their museum had sample rooms of how the nuns lived in those days—very simple furniture with little or no comforts. But I noticed that the convent had been built so that one could look out on beautiful gardens and sky almost anywhere one happened to be, even coming down stairways. The cellar had many glass-covered coffins containing the skeletons of nuns. A few still had scraps of clothing on. I felt sorry that these ladies had to be thus exposed.

One could spend days in the acres of Chapultepec Park and the castle that once housed Maximilian. But there was one place which Fred thought we should not miss. (For my sake, I'm sure.) In a booklet called *A Guide to Mexican Poetry*, we had come across a description of Calzada de los Poetas. It described this Promenade of Poets as "a tranquil promenade, running southward from the Casa de Lago, beneath the cathedral-like arches formed by ancient ahuehuete trees. Along it are set the busts of Mexican poets."

We had carried the book with us, asking where it was over and over again. More than once we were misdirected, perhaps because our question was misunderstood; but at last we found it. The bronze busts were most interesting. And there were other promenades with busts of artists, composers, and philosophers. What a splendid way to honor such lovers of truth and beauty; where one can sit on benches in the quiet of trees and flowers and read their works or write one's own thoughts.

On Sunday morning, we took the bus back to the park just to have a walk in it, but found we had arrived on the day of celebration of the Boy Heroes, September 13, 1847. These very young cadets of the military academy installed in Chapultepec Castle had been abandoned to their fate when United States troops, under General Winfield Scott, occupied the city. The Boy Heroes were all killed trying bravely to withstand the invaders.

At the small amphitheater, not far from the Poets' Promenade, we were in time to hear a good part of a long poem read in parts by four men and four women, with a refrain spoken in unison. As they read, they moved to different levels of the stage. How we wished we could understand Spanish! No one could possibly miss the emotion, but it was not overdone. We tried in vain to find out the names of the poem and the poet.

There were well over two thousand people listening when we arrived, and more and more kept coming. All were intensely interested and so quiet you could hear a leaf drop. Most were everyday people like us—parents and grandparents, young couples, children, farm families, city families, a gang of young boys, pairs of lovers —all listened, enthralled.

Fred was more determined than I was to trace down

the name of the long poem read at the celebration; not that I wasn't interested, but you all know that your father has a lot more stick-to-itiveness than I have. At last a paper boy in the hotel lobby suggested we try the office of the city's largest newspaper, *Novedad.* We finally found the English-speaking editor on the third floor, who told us that the poem was indeed the famous "Boy Heroes," written by Amado Nervo. He lived from 1870 to 1919 and was not only a best-beloved poet, but also ambassador to Argentina, Uruguay, and other Latin-American countries.

As a final splurge, we went to dinner at the posh Hotel Cortez. This just had to be a dream. I kept thinking of our past—China, war, concentration camp, India. By the farthest stretch of the imagination, we had never pictured ourselves in our late sixties sitting under the stars in the romantic courtyard of a Spanish Colonial monastery (formerly), wood fires burning on the old bricks to keep off the chill, we two holding hands as the musicians played!

The fountain had been covered to become a stage where three dancers from the Ballet Folklórico performed. In a corner behind shrubs, a marimba band played (three marimbas and two percussion instruments). This band alternated with a mariachi band in Spanish costumes. The food was superb. What an evening! What an ending to our wonderful vacation!

Home late, through Alameda Park, where the singing and dancing there had stopped and only the lovers were left.

We love you, each one,
Mom

EIGHT

We came to the end of an era with the publication of *The Happiest Summer,* the story of the marriage of Judy, our last child to leave home. Sad as it was to say the farewells, to come home to an empty house, "with not one pair of shoes under any of the chairs," as Fred noted, it is now an overwhelming joy to have the children all in their own homes, happily married and with children of their own. There is no way to express our gratitude for such undeserved blessings.

And how we love our visits to them and theirs to us. Son Jim, a reporter for *Newsday,* his wife Dixie, and their Jessica and Elizabeth are on Long Island. Son Carl, his wife Faith, and their Helen, Christopher, and Rebecca are in Boston, where Carl is the minister of King's Chapel. Daughter Anne, her husband John Fitch, part-time minister and full-time school administrator, and their David, Andy, and Lorrie are in Saranac Lake, where Anne is executive director of American Red Cross for that area. Son Tom, his wife Janene, and their Derick and Daw Rung (the little adopted granddaughter they brought us from Thailand) are in

Pittsburgh, Pennsylvania, where Tom is associate professor of linguistics at the university and Janene is teaching in the public schools. Daughter Judy, her husband John Robinson, and their Elizabeth and Joy are living in England, John's birthplace. John carries on a teaching program for apprentices in factories covering a large sector of England in the London area. Daughter Vicki, her husband Jim Harris, and their Michael and Laura Judith live in one of the new suburbs of Chicago, not too far from O'Hare Airport. Jim has a position with National Car Company.

I have designated "son" and "daughter" for clarity only. Recently someone seeking advice asked if I did not think it wise on breaking up a home after the death of parents to have only the "blood" children present— not those who had married into the family. I told her that I never thought of the six whom our six had brought home to us as being in a different category from the "originals." (Not long ago I came across a line in my diary written the night Judy's husband-to-be arrived from England for the wedding. It read, "Our last son has come home.")

This does not mean that we expect them to feel the same way about us, especially at first. They have (or had at the time) parents of their own to whom they feel very close. A second set of parents takes a bit of getting used to. Some had the added difficulty of not even seeing their Scovel in-laws until years after their marriage, as we were still with the Mission overseas.

When I first came into the Scovel family, Fred's mother told me that ever since he was a little boy, she had been praying for the one who would be growing up to become his wife. I decided to do this for our children, too. Perhaps that is why I felt as if I had always known them when we first saw them.

People sometimes ask us what we did in bringing up our children that "made them turn out so well." We reply that it must be something in their genes. They are fortunate in having good, strong, God-fearing grandparents and great-grandparents for generations back. We know parents who have done as much or more for their children than we have, and who have had unexplainable tragedies. We can only say that we tried, and that we loved them very much and let them know that. Fred usually adds, "We prayed a lot, too." And we still do, as do millions of other parents. The prayer I use each day for all of us I learned as a child in the Episcopal Church in Mechanicville, New York:

Dear Lord, our heavenly Father, who hast safely brought us to the beginning of this day; defend us in the same by thy mighty power; and grant that this day we fall into no sin, neither run into any kind of danger; but that all our doings, being ordered by thy governance, may be righteous in thy sight; through Jesus Christ our Lord. Amen.

Heredity is a factor over which we have no control. No one of us can be sure what our genes will come up with next. But we can be sure of prayer. It is up to us as parents and grandparents to make the most of what we have received and to hand it on to those for whom we are responsible. If we have been unfortunate enough to have missed the kind of a home we wish we might have had, it is not too late to set new patterns for our children to hand down to theirs.

Our children are especially blessed with an understanding, sympathetic father. In a family argument, they invariably took his side. There were times when I felt they were all teaming up against me, no doubt rightfully so because (maddeningly) he is usually right.

I have never thought of myself as having been a good mother, and perhaps, like all mothers, I wish I had it to do over again. I would like to have known a great deal more about child-rearing than I knew then. I would like to have had more time to treat each one as an individual instead of en masse. The only way to be a perfect mother is to have already brought up each child, then to have the opportunity to do it over again. Impossible, of course, but we mothers can comfort ourselves in the thought that our children also learn from us what *not* to do in bringing up their children.

There has always been a lot of laughter in our house. We save jokes and cartoons and stories to tell one another. And, as in most families, we "remember when . . . ," for instance, Tom collected all the dolls and took them to the roof of our three-storied house in India, then floated them down by parachutes made from his father's handkerchiefs to the two screeching, crying sisters below.

"And it wasn't funny either," Judy and Vicki will add to this day.

We recall and use Judy's special vocabulary, "It dissesappears." "It snew," for "It snowed." Things like radishes "snorked" her nose.

We never know what may happen in our house. One night Fred and I were tired and depressed from a more than usually difficult day in New York. We said nothing about it to teen-age Vicki. She went upstairs, we thought, to do her homework. But down she came, dressed as a bona fide flapper of our youth—her dress a floor-length red flannel nightgown, pulled up very short by a tight belt. She wore long strings of beads, a ribbon around her head, and was chewing gum, dancing the Charleston and singing, "Has Anybody Seen My Gal?" She went on performing until we ached from laughing.

We remember how, as children, Jim and Carl sat at their desks, back to back, drawing sketches and cartoons to illustrate the stories they were composing as they went along. As soon as one sheet was finished, it was discarded and a new sheet started, with no interruption to the story. Many a wastebasketful was thrown out in the course of an afternoon. How I wish we had saved a few choice specimens!

Often the boys were interrupted by their little sister, Anne, intent on recognition even if it were teasing to the point of tears. Replays of the scene in present-day settings are played to a delighted family audience. Here is Anne at our home with her husband and three children; Jim and Carl arrive with their families, and in no time the Director of the American Red Cross is notifying me that the *Newsday* Reporter and the Boston Minister "are teasing me."

Having children forces you into thinking of someone else besides yourself. Marriage does, in a way, but not when you have a husband who spoils you at every turn. I have a great propensity for self-centeredness, and he doesn't help to make me any less so. But having a first baby breaks open a new world—a world in which there is someone so dependent upon you that you must think of that someone every waking moment and a good share of the sleeping ones. Having six children, with all their separate horizons, stretches you far beyond yourself and there is little time for much else.

Being a writer takes you back into self-centeredness again. You are in a little world of your own making, cocooned by an insulation that shuts out any thought of others. Your self and what you are doing assume an importance which is out of all proportion to reality. You become in your own eyes a very important person, entrusted with thoughts so great that they are of interest to the whole world. No one else can write them. No other person has ever before or ever will have this particular revelation.

Knowing that this has not come *of* you but *through* you—that the gift can be taken away as easily as it was given—you are under pressure to get thoughts on paper and to the world, lest they be lost. You resent any intrusion, even by loved ones, until what you feel you have been given to write has been completely expressed as well as you are able to do it.

I am grateful for the gift and more than grateful for the children. And I am thrice glad to have been a given a consuming interest now that the children have found their mates, have their homes and families, and are happily looking out on their own horizons.

The days of our child-rearing are over and we do not say it sadly. We are glad to be alone together, to feel that we have done a job good enough for the children to stand on their own feet. They are entirely capable of managing their lives and of making their own decisions. And we are pleased at what these decisions have been.

NINE

We do not plan to live with our children. We have joked about this for years, telling them that the reason we had six was so that when we retired we could live two months with each one every year, thinking that when they had been through that experience for about two years, they would get together and buy us a house of our own. Now that won't be necessary as we already have our home, and they are off the hook! However, we are repeatedly given the assurance that if the time comes when we feel like changing our minds, we will not be left out in the cold.

We hope that time will not come, for their sakes, for our sakes. I was sixty-two years old when our last child was married. This meant thirty-nine years of mothering. I would not have missed one of them. And I have a wealth of clever and amusing stories of talented grandchildren, such as Rebecca, squatting in the road, feeding animal crackers to the black man and the white man working in the manhole, and . . . well, there are limits to the pages of this book. I dearly love each one of our fourteen grandchildren, but I have not been the kind of a grandmother who is always on hand to baby-sit. Our children have been most understanding about thirty-nine years being enough.

One treat I have not missed is being with our daughters after the birth of their children. The birth itself is for man and wife to go through together. I arrived the day after or even a bit later. Ever since my days as a pediatric nurse, I have adored newborn babies. Joy for me is to feel their small bodies relax against my shoulder. I even like to soothe them during colic spells. But as grandmother to a new baby, I feel that my main job is to assume the burden of housework and meals so that the mother can regain strength and be free to enjoy the care of the little one.

We do not live near enough to any of our children to be running in on them or to have them dropping in on us. Some days I long for it. But proximity has its advantages and disadvantages. Having a mother or mother-in-law in the house or appearing at unexpected moments can present difficulties.

No one could have had a better mother-in-law than I had. And she had a remarkable influence on our children's lives for which any parent would be most grateful. She read to them by the hour—the usual children's books plus Thackeray, Dickens, and other classics, explaining the plot as she went along. She had each one separately for lunch during the short time she had a house alone. What a boon when a child feels lost in a busy household of not only brothers and sisters but houseguests (mostly relatives of patients in the hospital. There were no rooming houses or hotels or motels where we lived).

"When it comes to discipline, I never interfere," Mother Scovel would say. It was true that if I were scolding a child, she would not say a word. But she couldn't help looking across at him or her with that expression of deepest sympathy which all but said: "Never mind, dear. I know she is cross, but I'll make it up to you as soon as she is finished."

Just recently, I found myself in the same predicament and with the same look on my face, I am sure.

Having another person in the house makes a lot of difference. Mother lived with us for fourteen years. She gave me beautiful gifts which I treasure. She stayed with the children and their amah in the rare instances when Fred and I both had to be away on a medical trip in the country. She did lovely, thoughtful things for all of us and did not interfere with our plans or decisions. But for the full fourteen years, I never made one decision, however small, without wondering, What will Mother say? Though I can honestly affirm that I have never once wished I had not suggested that we ask her to live with us after Father died. Yet there were times when it was not easy for her or for us.

But there are families where every marital difficulty is taken at once to the mother or mother-in-law, or she is present to hear the arguments leading up to it. It is all but impossible not to take sides. Too often what might have been a moment's "scrap" becomes an ever-increasing breach. Fred and I both feel strongly that husbands and wives and their children need to be alone as a family if that is at all possible.

The ghost of my three greats Italian grandmother may haunt me for this. Italian families, especially mothers, insist on as much proximity as possible. Daily visits are expected, or at least weekly for the all-important Sunday dinner. Otherwise the mother feels hurt and neglected.

There is another side. I have known parents of our age who wish they did not have to keep the earlier patterns. They long to be left alone without having to spend year after year taking care of grandchildren and week after week cooking that Sunday dinner (even if others in the family help). They long for the son to go off and get married so his wife can pick up after him, do his washing, and have his meals ready on time. But they would not dare say so for fear of "what people might say."

We remember the afternoon when we were out for a drive and suddenly realized that we did not have to be home in time to get supper for anybody. And there was no one worrying about where we were or why we didn't come. We could go on farther, eat out, or even stay all night if we wanted to.

Best of all, our children seem to enjoy the fact that we are having such a good time alone.

We cannot always plan our own lives. Emergencies come to all of us and the course of our lives is changed. Then we do what we have to do and pray for God's strength to see us through.

And one does not ever want to cut one's self off from the children. There are times when they need us and want us and there are times when we need them. But after marriage, it is not good for them to become too dependent upon us, nor for us to become too dependent upon them.

When we first got home from overseas and the children came for visits, we were surprised to see a slight returning to their childhood—the girls, not the boys. They and their father had been men together since they were toddlers. But the girls slipped into "Mommy," instead of "Mom." I was amused to find the same little pouts when I woke them up in the morning. They had missed and now asked for their father's arms around them.

This was not their fault. I too was treating them like children. They were annoyed or amused, depending on which daughter it was, at my pushing them away from the roast in the oven with, "Here, let me do that. You'll burn yourself," forgetting that they had arrived with their arms full of baked goods, which they had done in their own ovens, leaving no scars. It was hard for me to realize that they were women, not children.

Perhaps that was why their husbands became a bit uncomfortable as time went on, restless to be doing something important, or perhaps wanting to be in their own home where they were in control, the master of their own house, wanting her to be a wife again, not somebody's daughter.

All of this straightened itself out when I began to treat them all as persons to be loved, not children to be managed.

No pleasure on earth can equal watching one's children and theirs grow up. It is such joy to be living in the same country with most of them and to be able to travel to the one still overseas. We are thankful, too, to be living once more in our homeland. I am back on my own schedule of writing, and Fred is off to work at the hospital. He couldn't be happier than to be with patients again. And he can leave at night without worrying, since he is a consultant and the staff doctors are in full charge of the patients.

As for administration, he came home one afternoon, threw himself down in his leather chair, and with a grin as wide as a split watermelon, said, "They're having an executive committee meeting. Ha! Ha! Ha!"

TEN

One afternoon in early summer, as we were drinking our lemonade under the beech tree, I said to Fred, "If you could do anything you wanted to do, go any place, buy anything, fulfill any dream, what would it be?"

"What in the world made you ask that question?" he wanted to know.

"Time is running out on us and whatever we're going to get or do before we die, better be got or done," I replied.

"Cheerful thought," said Fred. "Is that a goldfinch in the birdbath?"

A few days later, he said, "In answer to that question of yours the other afternoon, I can't think of a thing I would want that I haven't got except to have you learn to drive the car."

Well! I'd asked for it and I had my answer—the last one I wanted to hear. How many times in the past had he spoken of it? I thought that by now he had given up the idea.

"But I like being chauffeured, especially by you," I told him.

"It was your idea that time was running out. What if I go first?"

"Then I'd have to learn to drive, I suppose."

"By then you might be too old to get a license. Honey, you asked me and that's all I can think of that I really want."

I knew he would say no more about it, and I knew that this was something I was going to have to do. I had had a warning the previous summer. The night before we were to leave Big Moose Lake, Fred had a gallbladder attack and had been in pain for hours. I begged him to stay over another day and not try to drive the long trip home, but he insisted. Those five hours were a nightmare as his driving was anything but his usual careful, expert handling of the car. I thought then, If I had learned to drive the car when I was younger, this wouldn't have had to happen.

Now he was saying that it was all he wanted from life. It was up to me to get busy.

I am awed by engines, machines, anything mechanical. Fred would say, "She can't even change an electric light bulb." Once, years before, I had taken a few lessons at an evening class in the local high school. Nothing ever came of it, perhaps because we were in New York weekdays, and Saturdays were used up doing housework and shopping. More likely, it was because I did *not* want to learn to drive. Now there was no way out.

My first teacher couldn't believe that anyone my age had not driven a car at some time in her life. He showed me how to start the engine, told me to go ahead down the road, up a steep hill to the town's main street, around a couple of blocks, then down an even steeper hill right into the fast-moving, home-going evening traffic of the main highway.

I made it home, walked into the house on legs of jelly, and collapsed on the sofa for a good cry. The second lesson might never have been taken if it hadn't been for a line from my morning devotions written by Robert O. Laaser, which I had cut out and happened to run across just in time: "Real toughness is not winning victories; it is not giving in to defeats" (From *These Days* magazine, May-June 1971).

After several more lessons, I did change schools, which turned out to be a very wise move.

Two and a half years, some sixty-five plus lessons, five tests, and one broken garage door later, I received my permanent license. I didn't say a word when Fred came home that day, but left the letter on top of his pile of mail and went on pouring coffee. When he opened it, he jumped up from the table, threw his arms around me, and said: "Congratulations! Oh, honey, I'm so glad. Now I can have my coronary in peace."

I assured him that that had not been exactly what I'd had in mind when I undertook the project.

It was a tremendous satisfaction to be able to say to myself, "Mission accomplished." But it was without question the most difficult thing I have ever done. I, who had always slept like a hibernating bear, was losing a lot more than forty winks. When I did manage to get to sleep, I would wake up shivering with fear that I might cause an accident or hit a child. I still shudder even to think of those nights. When I was driving, I did not feel nervous, and soon came to enjoy it.

Failing the driving tests was discouraging and humiliating. All my life, things had come easily; now I was having failure after failure. But bad as I felt about it, I knew that the failures were a learning experience which was good for me. A colleague of Fred's at the hospital wrote a sympathetic note:

Dear Myra,

I heard from Fred that you are again taking your road test. I know how you feel, but remember that *highly* sensitive, creative, intelligent people fail it several times.

Good luck!

Flattery, yes. But how encouraging to one who was feeling old and incompetent!

And one night, our granddaughter Helen phoned to read me a section from the *Guinness Book of World Records*. A certain Mrs. Hargrave of Yorkshire, England, aged sixty-two, had passed on her fortieth driving test. Thanks to Helen, from then on I did not hem or haw when people asked, "Have you got your license yet?"

I simply replied, "I only have to take thirty-six (or whatever) more to beat the Guinness World Record of failures." Immediately, the subject changed to dear Mrs. Hargrave.

I hadn't dreamed that our children would be so enthusiastic. One after another they wrote of how proud they were that I would even attempt such a thing at seventy-two. No mother could help feeling encouraged. When the tests came around, they phoned to cheer me on, assuring me of their prayers. Anne did not tell me until later that she was praying I would not pass until I was fully able to drive safely. She had received her license before she had any confidence in herself, and did not want me to drive with such fear as she had had.

"Do you think I was terrible?" she asked.

"Not at all. I was praying the same thing myself," I told her.

Fred, as always, upheld me every step of the way. He is an excellent teacher, and I was glad to have him between the two driving schools. But the old Matador, without power steering, was more than I could conquer. By the time I had practiced three or four turns, the old tendonitis in my upper arms would flare up, and I couldn't drive again for several days.

"What will I do now?" I moaned. "It isn't going to do any good to learn to drive when I can't manage our own car."

"We'll just have to get a new car with power steering," said Fred.

"But you planned to keep the car for the rest of the year. Besides, you don't like power steering."

"A few months won't make that much difference; we've got the money saved. And I'll get used to power steering eventually."

The result was our beautiful little brown-gold Pacer. The car was made for us. At last I could see the road without sitting on a pile of sliding pillows. And though I was practically up to the dashboard on the driver's side, there was still plenty of room for Fred to stretch his long legs on his side. I had always thought of the car as being Fred's and I still do—except when I am driving alone. What a delicious feeling of confidence and independence!

And what a thrill it was to surprise son Tom! He had come to the Stony Point Center to take part in a meeting and would spend the night with us. I drove over to pick him up. He came running out of the building, but stopped dead still when he saw me at the wheel. "Mom! I can't believe it! It looks so strange to see you sitting there!"

And how I glowed when I heard him say, "Dad, Mom can really drive!"

And his father's reply, "Of course! She's a very good driver."

"He who endures to the end shall be saved."

But I have one admonition—learn to drive young. And if it's too late for that, don't put it off till you are an hour older.

ELEVEN

I once overheard a daughter-in-law asking a daughter what she could give us for Christmas.

"Anything that they can eat or that will self-destruct," was the reply.

By the time a couple reaches the Golden Wedding Anniversary (and long before!), the accumulation of *things* is apt to have filled every crevice. And this, for us, after losing two complete households of everything except what we had on our backs—one set to the Japanese Army and one to the Chinese Communist Army. We still go to the shelves for books we know we have but haven't.

After two such sweeping losses, how can it be that our house is again filled to overflowing, even after the patronage of church fairs, rummage sales, and helping six families get started? True, "Nature abhors a vacuum," but how does she manage to fill it so quickly? Every once in a while, Fred looks around and says, "We need another war."

And I reply, "There has to be a better way."

Mother Scovel's furniture and Chinese curios were

spared. After she died, the Chinese Government allowed us to ship them to America. These are the cherished pieces we are using now. They are only things, we know, yet they are rich with memories for all of us.

The big question is, What to do with them? How divide them equally among six families? Should we do it now or leave it all for the children to do later? Not one of them would quibble, but is it fair to put them in this position? In every family there are those who would find it hard to give up anything, not because they are greedy, but because it would mean so much to have what was in their childhood home. Others already have their homes furnished to their taste, and there would be little space for any additions; a curio, a favorite picture, or a vase, perhaps, but which one to which family? And what about the ones who will want a certain item but will say, "Go ahead, take it," and think, "Anything to keep peace in the family." How, then, can an estate be divided fairly? The one favorite vase may turn out to be more valuable than everything else put together.

There will be a few items that have already been designated years earlier. Our beloved Cousin Harriet has specified that the Victorian love seat is to go to Tom and Janene when we no longer need it. The grandfather clock from Mother Scovel's family, the Kiehles, was left to Fred for our lifetime, then is to be passed on to our oldest son, James Kiehle Scovel. The carved bamboo figure of Lao Shou Hsing was Vicki's "doll" which, when a child, she dressed, undressed and put to bed, the old gentleman smiling through it all. She claims she has "loaned it to us," and we cannot help agreeing.

These items should be written into our will, perhaps but we cannot see it all cluttered up with this-and-thats for so-and-sos, since the needs and wants of each of our beloveds may have changed completely before the will is read. Too, they may be living in distant countries where it would not be practical to ship heavy old pieces of furniture, as is even now the case in Judy's family.

Then there are the old photographs to be sorted, labeled, and the unknown relatives and friends discarded. And the files! We couldn't leave unsorted those metal drawerfuls, both mine and Fred's! It would make even the bravest and most curious of the clan quail to undertake the project. In such a case, it might be wise to throw everything out without looking. An even wiser way might be for Fred and me to go over everything now, asking ourselves, not "Am I ever going to use this again?" but "Can I possibly live without it?" And if that doesn't work, "How many years has it been since I've even looked at it?"

The all-important family records can be passed on any time and need not wait until we die.

There, I've said it. Though we are in our early seventies, with the possibility of twenty or even thirty years ahead of us, we *are* getting ready to die and we want to make our death as easy for our children as possible. (Or we *say* we do. The photos haven't been worked on for a couple of years and the files are still untouched.)

"Morbid," says Vicki. "I don't want you to think about death or talk about it at all."

I fully understand. She is young and it is not death she fears; it is separation. Thinking about it, I wonder if perhaps death is somewhat like going away to college. The child does not want to leave the warmth and security of home for the unknown that lies ahead, yet is terribly thrilled and excited to be off to an ever-widening horizon. And the family cannot bear to be separated from the child, yet knows that only by leaving can a richer life be gained. This knowledge does not ease the pain of separation. Perhaps it helps one to accept it.

But why is there such a taboo on talking about death? I am convinced that one doesn't fully appreciate life until one comes to grips with the fact that it is to happen to each of us—today, tomorrow, or years ahead. Realizing this may cause us to look around, to appreciate and enjoy each day as it comes. Earth is so beautiful and we pay so little attention to its beauty. We continue to go on defacing it, destroying it, counting it the very least among the things we are willing to pay to save. And in so doing, we are destroying ourselves.

It seems of little importance that the air we breathe is killing us. We want a car for every member of the family, and with each member working at a different job, it is impossible to do anything else. But we make no plans for changing the transportation systems so that this would not be necessary. We continue to buy more cars each year instead, then proceed to disconnect the antipollution devices so that we can kill ourselves more quickly.

We seem intent on ruining our environment, our planet Earth, of which, we are told, there is only this one of its like in the whole universe. If this is true, we are indeed a chosen people. One wonders if we should have been trusted with it.

Strange, that we go on working toward our own death, yet shy away from thinking or talking about it.

What would you do if it were your last day on Earth and you knew it? Why not pretend it is and take the day off?

What would I do? It would *not* be a day to rush into trying to finish the book; it would be too late for that. It would *not* be a hasty scramble to clear out the files and clean the house, and it would *not* be a day of last-minute prayers—the usual ones, perhaps, because it would be hard to get through any day without a time of prayer.

I like to think that for me, it would be a day of rest and joy and gratitude for all life has meant; a day to sit in the garden, smelling *Earth*, its soil, its fresh, clean flower fragrances. I'd want to touch the bark of trees, feel the softness of the rose petals, watch the growing things and the birds. (I count on its being spring, summer, or early autumn, you may have noticed.)

There is no fear in this hypothetical day, simply because it *is* hypothetical. And I doubt if there will be any fear when the real day arrives. There comes to mind a thought from *King's Chapel Newsletter,* which our son Carl was given by one of his parishioners. It is a quotation from Ugo Betti: "To believe in God is to know the rules will be fair and there will be wonderful surprises."

Meanwhile, there is the rest of our lives to live to the full. Now we are free to do all the things we always wanted to do, some of the things we have always known we should do, and lots of the things we never dreamed we'd do—not only the hard things such as learning to drive, but the fun things such as spending a day with Gertrude and Curtis and having a picnic in the park.

TWELVE

Rev. and Mrs. Frank Curtis Williams have been close friends of ours for many years. Whenever we meet, we begin at once to talk about our current interests. Mrs. Williams is known to her public as the poet and author Gertrude Ryder Bennett. (Her mother was also a poet who wrote under the name of N. M. Bennett.)

"What are you writing now?" is always a first question with us.

This time Gertrude answered, "I'm doing a book called *Living in a Landmark.*"

"I can't wait to see it," I told her.

I love their beautiful old home, a Dutch Colonial farmhouse, barn, garden, and orchard set down in the middle of—guess where? Brooklyn. Four generations of the Bennett family have lived in the house which is now a historical landmark. The old barn bears an inscription attesting to the fact that it has been standing since 1766. There are enough stories in that house to fill a tome.

Two of Gertrude's books, *Ballads of Colonial Days* and *The Fugitive* had given hints of this, and her long, authenticated story in poetry, *The Hessian Lieutenant*

Left His Name, removed all doubt. It tells of two Hessian officers quartered in the house during the Revolution. Each left his name inscribed on a windowpane.

"And what are you writing, Myra?" Curtis asked.

"I'm playing around with some ideas for another book about the family," I told him. "But this time I'm saving the children from a year or two of wondering, 'What is she saying about us now?' and concentrating on our retirement."

"Curtis is a past master at that," said Gertrude.

Rev. F. C. Williams, S.T.B., of the Reformed Church in America, retired after forty years only to take another pastorate. Up to the present, he has had six ministries in Reformed and Methodist churches, including two years as counselor in the Presbyterian-Reformed Exhibit at the 1964–1965 New York World's Fair. In between, he has supplied pulpits here and there as needed. He is also a concert cellist.

Neither he nor Gertrude has waited for retirement to pursue their many interests. Curtis played the cello professionally to put himself through college. We four agree that hobbies should begin early in life, so that the years, as they come, may be enriched, and as a preparation for the years ahead.

"How did you become interested in printing?" I asked. For the next two hours, I pumped them with questions.

At one of his churches, the Sunday school had a print shop and a print club organized for the boys. One family gave printing equipment to the club in memory of their son who was killed in World War II. Two retired printers taught the young club members and soon they were doing all the printing for church activities, including the Sunday bulletins, so a larger press was purchased.

As the years went by, the boys grew up, the printers who had taught them died, and for five years the press lay idle. Upon his retirement, the officials of the church offered the large press to Curtis. Not only did he set it up in his basement, he also purchased a smaller press and forty additional cases of type.

"Someone remarked that I had more letterheads than I had friends to make them for," said Curtis. "But I enjoy the creativity of setting them up in different styles."

Each step he took in developing this hobby widened into something more. He subscribed to *Printing News,* a graphic arts paper that keeps him in touch with exhibits and new resources. He attends monthly luncheon meetings of the Typophiles, a graphic arts club where he meets congenial friends, gets new ideas, and hears informed speakers on typography and design. He studies the field from paper to promotional ideas which, incidentally, can also be used in understanding how parishioners may react to new ideas.

"One step leads to another," said Curtis. "I happened to send a card with shaded letters to a lawyer and he wrote back asking, 'Who's your printer?' I told him I was. This resulted in an order for three thousand letterheads and envelopes."

"We had paper and envelopes laid out on every horizontal surface in the house," said Gertrude. "I'm his printer's devil. Isn't that what you'd call his apprentice?"

"We enjoy our hobbies together," said Curtis. "We call ours Willett Press—the combination of Williams and Bennett. And I guess you know about Willett Studios."

"Yes, but how did you get started on your ceramic hobby?" I asked.

"We were on a camping trip, going to a county fair in Vermont," said Gertrude. "I had taken along some shells to make some jewelry which I thought I might sell there. I also took a pound of clay (not the kind that has to be fired). We didn't know a thing about using it, but we thought we'd both learn.

"On the way back, we stopped at a place where the sign read, 'Wagon Wheel Studio, Ceramics, Lessons.' There we met Vicki Hoffman, who not only gave us lessons but fed us! We came home raring to get started. We had enough pieces of what we had already learned to show to another ceramist, Adelle Carlough, and she continued our lessons.

"We also learned ceramic decorating—the hard way," Gertrude went on.

"It was Christmastime and Adelle had an order for grosses and grosses of small china eggcups with a rooster and a hen painted on each one. Adelle had lost her decorator and I pitched in to help. I painted day and night until I never want to see another eggcup, but we filled the order on time. She paid me for my work and we bought a kiln, which opened another phase of ceramics—the firing. And having learned to paint on china led to still another hobby, decorated ceramic jewelry, tiles and pictures, then to sculptures of small animals to mount on rocks we collect from quarries."

I was being rushed from one hobby to another so fast I was running out of breath. But the "Willetts" were not through yet.

On one of their camping trips in the Adirondacks, they had come upon the Barton Mine at North Creek. There, Gertrude picked up a small black rock with something in it which sparkled. It was just what she wanted for mounting a ceramic she had made—a small coyote, baying at the moon. The black rock was hornblende, and when they learned that the sparkles were garnets, and that they were, in fact, at a garnet mine, one more hobby was born—collecting semiprecious stones. This took them to other mines: to Herkimer for the beautiful crystals called Herkimer Diamonds, to Saranac Lake for moonstones and a Rock Swap.

"People back their cars in a circle, leaving the trunks open so they can show their rocks, something like the pioneer wagons around a campfire," said Gertrude.

"We meet many fine people on these trips," said Curtis. "There was a small child at Saranac who offered thirty-five cents for a rock worth much more than that. No one offered a higher bid."

"We have some strange experiences, too," said Gertrude. "Once we saw a sign that read 'Rock Swap, Windsor, Maine.' When we got there, we could find no place to stay, so we went to Rumford and stopped at 'Wild Animal Park.' In the middle of the night, I was awakened by the roaring of a lion. It was such a ferocious noise that I was frightened to death. What if it got loose? What if it *was* loose?"

While in Maine they panned for gold (and got one tiny nugget). They picked up rubies in the mines of North Carolina. In Patrick County, Virginia, they found the strange stone cross formations called staurolites. All this led to lectures—a slide program in which Curtis spoke on "Adventures in Mining" and Gertrude came on bedecked with examples of the specimens they had made into jewelry.

"You might say our camping out is another of our hobbies," said Gertrude.

They travel in a Volkswagen bus with a bed on each side, leaving an aisle down the middle. They are equipped with everything they need—sleeping bags, blankets, drinking water (for places where they are not sure the water is safe), thermos bottles, a hibachi, a woodbox for chips and charcoal, kitchen utensils, a week's supply of food. And there is still room to move about, to sit and eat, or to write.

"Then do you work on your books or poems on these trips?" I asked.

"Not unless something comes spontaneously," she replied. "Then I jot down the idea and carry it through as it comes, but I don't work on it until I get home. I do keep a diary, not only a log of the trip, but ideas, thoughts, and reactions."

Their travels as Gertrude researches her books take them far and wide. She talked about the summer she was working on *The Hessian Lieutenant Left His Name.* They followed the route taken by the Hesse-Hanau Artillery during the Revolution—in Canada, down Lake Champlain, all over the eastern part of New York State, New England, to Newport.

"Once we were camping at Arcadia State Park," said Gertrude. "There we met an Indian woman who said: 'We're having a powwow tomorrow. Won't you come to lunch with us?' So we did, and we've been going to powwows ever since."

"You two have such a good time living. Do you have any advice for the rest of us on how to retire?" I asked.

"Curtis is the one to tell you that," said Gertrude. "He is writing an article on 'The Art of Retirement.' I would say, 'Live life to the fullest.' 'The Kingdom of God is within you.' That's what He meant—that full, rich, abundant life within *is* the Kingdom."

"It is 'the Way, the Truth, the Life,'" Curtis went on. "We must love the very idea of the full Life pulsing through us. Christ said, 'Except ye become as a little child . . .' Children are excited about life, about everything."

"And start very early to become interested in all life has to offer," said Gertrude. She glanced at her watch. "We really must go. Oh, did I tell you that I collect antique postcards of Brooklyn and Coney Island?"

And she makes all her own clothes and many of her hats!

THIRTEEN

Dearest Children,

Sorry to be so late in getting this to you.

Everything went perfectly on our oh-so-restful Pan Am flight, both ways. What a luxury to be able to read for five hours with Fred beside me to share things with! But to start with the beginning: Our dear son-in-law was waiting at the London airport and the ride from there to Henlow by car took about an hour and a half. What a thrill it was to see Judy with the babe in her arms and dear little Elizabeth waiting for us! Of course we had to sit down for a cup of coffee and Judy's freshly baked cookies.

Elizabeth was so much fun. She has quite a vocabulary for a three-year-old, and comes out with such unexpected things. If she didn't understand immediately, she said, with a rising inflection, "Pardon?" (pronounced paadon). And the first morning, Joy smiled at me! She is adorable, really a large baby for such a few weeks, healthy-looking, with rosebud lips and lovely features. One of the greatest joys of being there was feeling that small body against me as I held her.

But there were so many joys! Elizabeth and I had many a walk, picking tiny, inch-high daisies growing in the grass, very fragrant. We would stop to smell them every few feet. The days were summer bright and windy. Everyone has a garden, if it's only two feet square. Most are much larger. In bloom were wallflowers, iris, tulips, lilacs, rhododendron, pansies, forget-me-nots, and a host of small flowers I had never seen before. And of course, primroses.

Fred and I often walked across the fields to Henlow village. The old church stands out above everything else and can be seen from far away. It was built in A.D. 1100 and the ancient stone gives the edifice a look of warmth. The Robinsons worship here and, of course, so did we. The local stores are good, especially Mr. Bonner's grocery. His people are so kind and friendly. They welcomed us and were glad, for Judy's sake, that we had come. They have made her feel very much at home. The women looked so fresh and pretty in their pink silk coats over flowered dresses.

But I must tell you about Judy's home. The house is well built and comfortable—central heating (for those of you who were worried about our being cold). A front hall leads through to the kitchen, the stairway on the left as you come in. On the right, the living room with a fireplace. It becomes John's office evenings and Judy's piano-teaching studio daytimes. The kitchen has an electric stove, lots of cupboards, a washing machine and a drier so Judy can cook while doing the laundry. As you know, she is a great cook. We had gourmet food every day, but not too "way out," just very delicious.

Outside the dining room's glass door, there stretches a large lawn, flower beds on three sides, with Elizabeth's small hummock of a garden in the middle. I wish you could see her running around the lawn, talking to unseen people, playing by herself so imaginatively.

Beyond is the vegetable garden, John's delight. He was planting squash, cucumbers, radishes, green beans, corn, potatoes, green peppers, and lots more. "Experiments to see what grows best," he told us. The small plot will have its work to do to support all he plans to try. He enjoys it so much—can't wait to get off the business suit (though handsome he looks in it) and get into his gardening togs for the stint before dinner and then until dark, when his office work begins. He works very hard, but seems to enjoy his life, and manages to spend time with his family weekends, evenings, and early mornings.

One day Fred and I took the train to London and spent the day in the British Museum. My bag was searched before we were allowed to enter, by very gentlemanly, jovial guards. Bags and coats were then checked, and Fred and I proceeded, each on our own. I knew I would hold him up, since I can't stand as long as he can, and we each had special things we wanted to see—Fred, the philatelic department, the coin curator, and so forth. I began with holographs.

It was very moving to read the journal of Captain R. F. Scott on his ill-fated South Polar expedition (1910–1912).

> We shall stick it out to the end, but we are getting weaker of course and the end cannot be far. It seems a pity but I do not think I can write more—
>
> R. Scott

Last entry—"For God's sake look after our people." A happier find was a sonnet titled "Shakespeare," in the handwriting of Matthew Arnold, which I copied out. A note written by Samuel Taylor Coleridge (1772–

1834) tells of his writing the poem *Kubla Khan*. It ends with this explanation:

> This fragment with a great deal more, not recoverable, composed in a sort of Reverie brought on by two grains of opium, taken to check dysentry [his spelling] at a Farm House between Porlock & Linton, a quarter of a mile from Culbone Church in the fall of the year, 1797.

Louis Untermeyer tells of the "not recoverable" part as being because he was "unfortunately called out by a person on business from Porlock" who detained him for an hour. When he got back, he had some vague recollection of the "purpose and the vision" but could only write "eight or ten scattered lines."

On the way to a watercolor exhibition of old Punjabi Hills artists, I met a young, well-dressed woman, with a beautiful English complexion, whom I stopped to ask the way.

She smiled and said, "Aren't you Myra Scovel?"

I gasped out a "yes," and looked at her again— Nancy Staub, who was my boss's secretary while I was working in New York. She is now manager of the Metropolitan Museum in New York, in England on a busman's holiday, a museum, of course.

The famous Rosetta stone has a mysterious aura around it. This slab of black basalt was found in July 1799, not far from Rashid, Egypt. According to one account, it was found lying on the ground, and according to another, it was built into a very old wall. A company of French soldiers had been ordered to remove the wall in order to make room for a fort. Fortunately, the French Officer of Engineers noted that it bore three different scripts, and rightly supposed that they were three different versions of the same text. When the texts were compared and translated, the whole secret (up to that date) of the meaning of Egyptian hieroglyphics became decipherable!

When I remarked to the clerk from whom I bought a booklet about the stone, "What a miracle it was that the officer recognized its worth!" she replied, "It was meant to be."

One afternoon, John took us all to Woburn Abbey, the estate of the Duke of Bedfordshire, where wild animals roam the three thousand acres, and the public is allowed to see them close up. (Too close up to suit me!) The animals are very beautiful, except for two hippopotamuses the size of young trucks, who, though they smiled as they came out of their wallow, could hardly be called beautiful. The rhinoceroses aren't in that category either. But the lions, tigers, bears, monkeys, elands, even the wildebeests (gnus, to you—no pun intended) looked ever so much more beautiful here than they do in zoos. Some of them walked leisurely across the road immediately in front of us, as did peacocks, wild ducks, flamingos, and ostriches. Many wild pheasants dropped down on the green, too. The bears kept their distance, climbing trees to drape over a limb.

I wonder how an English beech tree felt when a lion first scratched its back on its bark. And speaking of beech trees, on the return trip John stopped for us to see "a bluebell woods"—a sight I will never forget. The mass of flowers is so thick that the blue lies like an aura just above them, and this extends as far back as one can see.

Our next trip was to see Dr. Eileen Snow, who, you remember, was director of the Medical College when we were in India; and of course, her sister Olive, whom you know as Dove.

For years they have been urging us to come to England and they did a lot to make this the wonderful trip it was. Books were waiting for us, an excellent map of the Bedfordshire area, and so forth.

What a glorious reunion we had at Forge House, West Alton, Hampshire! We met Dorothy, the eldest sister, who is a remarkable woman—was headmistress of a girls' school for years, has a theological degree and a science degree.

We loved their renovated and restored seventeenth-century house with its old family furniture, added rooms, a marvelous kitchen, and from every window, green fields stretching away to the horizon. In a small, adjacent building is the weaving house where, once a week, Dorothy teaches a class in weaving. She also has three spinning wheels and spins her own yarns.

This must be among the oldest historical parts of England. We could see the breastworks of an old Roman fort, and across the soft green hills and out to sea, the Isle of Wight. It was a strange feeling to be walking along the road where Roman feet had trod; then came the Jutes, then the Anglo-Saxons who arrived by ship at what is now Southampton. Imagine walking through that very countryside! Eileen told us that, to this day, in the villages nearby, one sees the black-haired descendants of the Romans and the blond descendants of the Anglo-Saxons. As a rule, they do not intermarry.

Said Eileen, "You can get a haircut by Julius Caesar, Fred."

Charles the Second escaped down the road and the place where he hid was pointed out to us. The tales went on and on. And to bring history up-to-date, it was at Winchester, which we were approaching, that Churchill and Eisenhower, hiding in an old railway tunnel, planned the invasion of Europe.

Back at Forge House, we had tea and a wonderful

afternoon of poetry with Dove and another long-lost India friend, Eileen Ayers.

Time and your patience must be wearing out. When you come, we'll show you Fred's slides of Winchester and the great bronze statue of King Alfred the Great standing on a huge, rough boulder (which seems just right for it), and Winchester Cathedral and its arrangement of mirrors so that one can look down and see the stone arches of the ceiling high above—like a huge stone interior of an Adirondack guide boat. One of the stained-glass windows was given by Americans in 1938 as a tribute to "the life and character of King George V."

As you will see, Salisbury Cathedral is a contrast to the Norman architecture of Winchester. Its slim, ethereal spire seems to be in the act of rising above and away from the graceful Gothic structure. The windows were like jewels and as we looked down the aisles, the altar coverings of embroidery and tapestry appeared as distant flower arrangements. It was dear Dr. Dorothy Vaux, the pathologist from Ludhiana, who took us to the cathedrals—the artist. Remember?

Fred has done a pastel of Stonehenge which captures the deep quiet of those huge monoliths weighing tons and tons, set down in the middle of a meadow that stretches for miles. And they have been moved here from perhaps as far away as Wales. How could it have been done and by whom? The guidebook says, "We today can name no man or tribe who had all such qualifications at any time of British prehistory." Fred's pastel seems to have caught the mysterious quality of it.

It was noon and we went to our first pub to have a "ploughman's lunch"—slabs of delicious white bread, thick golden cheddar cheese, and beer. Of course, I had to spoil it all by ordering orange juice. No tea or coffee was available, and you know how I feel about beer.

The pub might have been a shot from a movie—complete with a British major who looked as if he had been chosen from hundreds as the perfect man for the part. He was a pleasant gentleman with one of the most beautiful dogs I have ever seen—a huge golden retriever, who made friends with Florence Collier's tiny dachshund named Patsy.

It was time to say farewell to the Snows and the friends who had given us so much of their time to show us their country. Now we were off on a mission we had looked forward to for years—in search of the land of your Scovel ancestors.

We went by train to Wareham, where we picked up a most interesting taxi driver named Keats. (Yes, he does trace his ancestry back to the poet. His vicar did it for him.) In a very short time, we were at our destination.

Corfe Castle is an amazing old village on the Isle of Purbeck, whence comes Purbeck stone used in both Winchester and Salisbury Cathedrals. By ordinance, no one can build a house in the village of any material except Purbeck stone. And the slate roofs are so heavy that, as the taxi driver said, "If a slab of it slipped as you were going past, it would cut your head off." We turned a corner and there above us were the gaunt, majestic ruins of the castle. Corfe is Anglo-Saxon for "gap," and the high, steep hill on which the castle stands rises at a gap in the mountain range which runs across the island. Surrounded by water at its base, the castle is so located that an approach from any direction could not be made without danger of showers of arrows or boulders from above.

For centuries it remained unharmed, but was destroyed by the Parliamentarians in 1646. They did a far more thorough job than was needed to keep it from becoming a fortress again. It is now impossible to tell what room was what, though the maps and diagrams give some information. The view was unbelievable, looking down on the lower hills covered with yellow gorse, and on out to sea. The wind almost whipped us off the hill.

Among the notes Fred brought along, there was a mention of "Scowel Farm." We asked the attendant at the gate if he had ever heard of it. He hadn't, but a young man painting nearby said: "Yes. Go straight through the village, up the Kingston hill. Halfway up, turn left into a farmhouse road and continue till you come to it. But it is *not* Scowel Farm; it is Scowel Manor." Well! Kingston was another village mentioned in one of the genealogies; so it is no doubt true that your Scovel ancestors did come from there. (Later, through correspondence with the occupants of Scowel Manor, we found it was indeed true and that there was a movement on foot to have the name changed to the correct spelling, Scovel.)

But time had run out. We were expected back in London. Our hosts, the Armitages, had invited some of our India friends for dinner. The taxi driver felt sure that he could find the way and that we could make it in record time. He tore up the road, around the bends, and up into the backyard of Scowel Manor. Fred jumped out, snapped a picture of the house with its sign to prove it, and we tore back down to the railway station. By running breathlessly, grabbing our luggage out of the checkroom, and running some more, we just made the train for London.

After a few more wonderful days with Judy and the babes, John was able to arrange time to take us all to his home in Sheffield. At last we were to meet his parents. Two cars were needed because of the baby's paraphernalia. (I just looked up that word in the dictionary and it means, "a married woman's personal possessions exclusive of her dowry.") I don't think that includes John's beautiful guitar, baby cart, etc., boxes of cookies and other foods, but at any rate, it all arrived intact.

What a warm, loving welcome we received! Jack and Dora are two of the dearest people in the world, and John's Grandmother Coombs is another. She has the bluest eyes I ever saw. Both she and Dora are much prettier than their pictures. Jack is a strong-looking, heavyset man with thick white hair. He is agile and full of interest in everything and everybody, lots of fun to be with. They both are. And such a fund of information Jack has on a variety of subjects.

I must admit that both Dora and I were a bit apprehensive about meeting, for fear we wouldn't know what to talk about. We practically fell into each other's arms and when it came time to leave, we both cried. And I don't think we stopped talking for any full minute we were together. It was as if we had always been relatives.

It would take months to tell you all we did—the trips to Derbyshire and the moors, a very quiet mysterious region of hills, great stone ledges, heather, peat, long stretches up and down dales. John had been a warden there, and knows the moors. They appeared to be so benign until he told us that "a woman died in a snowstorm, just over there, across the road from the pub. She was lost in the snow and got that close to civilization but didn't know it."

We ate delicious meals, had picnics, and a roast beef dinner with Dora's unsurpassable Yorkshire pudding! Sometime I hope you will each have a chance to meet that dear Robinson family. Meanwhile, we have some slides of them; also slides of family and friends we saw, some of whom you know and some you'll be introduced to for the first time, like Robin Gregory and his beautiful wife, Ann.

I have known him through correspondence and the poetry magazine *Orbis,* which he edits for the International Poetry Society. It had a poem of mine in the last issue, and he invited us to come to see them while we were in England. We had tea on the lawn and, of course, talked about poems and books. He and his wife had just finished a book on psychology for the layman. Others of his have been published by McGraw-Hill and other houses, but he is having the same trouble with this one that I am having with one of mine. It doesn't fit into any slot, so the publishers can't find a way to sell it, though all who have seen it agree the book is excellent and needed.

How grateful we are for these strong friendships which weather the years of separation and begin again as if it were yesterday!

As you well know, saying good-by to our children is the hardest thing that happens to me in this life (except learning to drive!). But I was ashamed to be sad because the visit had been so perfect. Judy and John had done so much for us and every moment with them and the children had been such a treat. We had a good flight home, found the house intact, and late as it was, we unpacked so we wouldn't have to live out of a suitcase one more day. Judy and John had had over a year of such living when they first got back to England from Iran. So we were all the more grateful to God for having seen them in their lovely home and to have been with them as they were settling in.

Love you, each one,
Mom

FOURTEEN

It happened suddenly and unexpectedly. I was checking out at a stationery store. On the counter were my boxes of manuscript bond, packages of manifold paper, carbons, paper clips, a dozen pens, and so forth. The look on my face, as the cost mounted, must have been a dead giveaway, for the man at the cash register said sympathetically, "If you will show me your Senior Citizens' card, I'll be glad to give you the discount."

With that one sentence, I not only became an old lady, I now knew I looked like one! As far as years were concerned, I was eligible, but I had no card, and we hadn't become members of our local Senior Citizens' Organization. It wasn't that we were unwilling to be counted among its one hundred seventy-five members, but that we were both too busy to take on anything more.

What I first noticed about our Senior Citizens was how well dressed they were and what a good time they seemed to be having. The women were among the first in town to wear the new pants suits, and in the whole gamut of the newest colors! The men were wearing the latest in trousers, sports jackets, shirts, and ties.

These people are on the go a good share of the time: trips to Quebec and Montreal, to Williamsburg and vicinity, to Mount Snow in Vermont, to Cape Cod, Martha's Vineyard, Plymouth, and Boston; five days and four nights at North Wildwood on the New Jersey shore; four days and three nights at Brown's Hotel in the Catskills; to Amish country in Pennsylvania, to the Danbury Fair in Connecticut, and so forth.

There are excursions to Shea Stadium to see the Mets play baseball; to the Belmont Racetrack, to Radio City Music Hall for the Easter and Christmas shows, followed by dinner at the Red Coach Grill. The reservations and arrangements for these outings are made by one of the women members. All the members take part in helping with every activity.

These men and women, some of whom might be sitting alone and feeling neglected, seem to be having more fun than all the rest of the town put together. At home in Stony Point, they celebrate every occasion—birthdays, Mother's Day, Father's Day, St. Valentine's Day, Fourth of July, St. Patrick's Day. This year the young students from the Immaculate Conception School entertained them with Irish dancing.

At their annual Anniversary Party, held at the Platzl Brauhaus, they entertain the Stony Point Town Council as an expression of their gratitude for their cooperation. In fact, it would be difficult to find an occasion that is *not* celebrated.

And it is not only themselves that these dear people are thinking of. Similar favors and place cards for each celebration are taken to the Rockland County Health Complex, the Helen Hayes Hospital, and Letchworth Village, so that the residents of these institutions may have their celebrations, too.

Forty-seven of our Senior Citizens also belong to the Retired Senior Volunteers Program (R.S.V.P.). Both organizations work hand in hand, members doing volunteer work and visiting. All pitch in to make, pack, and deliver the scores of cloth or wool lap robes, bed slippers, pillow cases, bibs made from old linen tablecloths; pocket bags for beds, walkers, and wheelchairs; hand-knit socks, and the like.

They find a use for everything one gives them. For instance, nylons no longer wearable because of runs are used for stuffing small, soft pillows to tuck in one's back, on which to rest an injured arm, or just to have handy.

Other organizations are not forgotten. Cash memorials are given to the Ambulance Corps. Cash and food items are given to the FISH program for the needy. Grocery coupons are saved for the Community Relations Office; Betty Crocker coupons are sent to Good Samaritan Hospital. Used postage stamps and tags from tea bags are saved for The Society of Mary. Used clothing goes to the Rockland County Infirmary.

We are proud to be citizens of a town that helps to provide such opportunities for its elderlies, and to be part of a community where citizens take advantage of such possibilities, not only for their own enjoyment, but by lightening the load of others.

It appears that there are those who know how to enjoy a life of retirement and those who enjoy so much the work they have been doing, or have recently had the opportunity to begin, that the day has not yet come when they want to leave it.

So it is for us . . . at present. But when the time comes, we will *not* be sitting at home feeling neglected. Not with all this going on in town.

FIFTEEN

So it was for two of our most beloved friends, Rev. and Mrs. J. Stewart Kunkle, for whom the time never came to cease working for the cause in which they believed. As long as we knew them, they were, and their memory continues to be, a joyous inspiration. How often we recall Julia's humor and Stewart's quiet smile, as well as their deep sensitivity and intellectual brilliance.

They had been missionaries in Canton long before we arrived. Julia went to China in 1913, where she served as teacher and librarian at Canton Christian College. Stewart was for years the president of Canton Union Theological College. They and their students were constantly uprooted by war. At one time, they trekked for days to a place where they could carry on their classwork free of interference, restrictions, and danger. They were robbed of all the money they had; their feet were bleeding, but on they walked. Food was scarce, but God provided.

A young missionary, a teacher from Wales, Rev.

P. W. Jones, later wrote his memories of these journeys.
In a letter to us after Julia's death, he said:

I have just written an account of Stewart and Julia in
the mountains above Kukong. I was with them from 1942
to 1944. The Kunkles and I were more than close friends,
and part of my getting down to this writing is so that this
extraordinary saga may not be forgotten. I don't suppose
they would even talk much about it, because they took
everything in stride, and in Julia's delightful humor. I can
still see her in a leaky room in a temple high in the mountains above Sin Yan Miu, all wrapped up in a blanket
because it was February and she had a cold.

The two servants shared the room and when I arrived
I was to get the floor space next to the door. We had eighty
students in the main temple and my two cows in the
broken-down room on the other side. I remember getting
a couple of the boys and hiking back down to the campus
among the big trees and bringing up a couple of rattan
chairs for the Kunkles to sit on. We had a party that night
and some of the students imitated each one of the staff in
turn, as they saw us. Later on, Julia asked me to recite the
Gettysburg Address for her. She knew it better than I did,
but she "liked my accent!" At that time, I heard stories
of how she and Stewart had met and how he had proposed
and she teased him a lot as he sat there and his eyes
twinkled blue.

Did you know he went through bandit areas lying in a
small boat all night to get to Canton for his wedding?
. . . Well, they won't ever die for me.

The Kunkles read prodigiously. A love of good books
flowed through both their bloodstreams. We often recall the time when Julia was making one of her trips to
New York with us.

"What are you going to do today, Julia?" I asked.
Her answer was a surprise, as usual. "Stewart has

given me a blank check for my birthday and has told me to buy all the books I want."

She came home with fourteen!

Books were not to be read, then retired to sit forever on shelves. The Kunkles believed that books were to be passed on. Lucky the person who happened in on a day when Julia decided to clear a bookcase. We were there one evening when she came to the conclusion that the valuable collection of books on China would be better off passed on to our children who had been born there.

As we went through the volumes, Fred and I sat on the floor in front of the bookcase; Julia, on a low chair beside us; Stewart, behind a newspaper nearby. We both tried to induce Julia to keep the most valuable books, to no avail. Suddenly Fred's face lighted up with surprise.

"Look at this," he said. "Here is a book written by one Julia Post Mitchell."

She reached to take it from his hand. "I'd forgotten it was there," she apologized.

Fred clung to the small volume, which turned out to be a study of the French writer, statesman, and agriculturalist, Jean de Crèvecoeur (1735–1813). He lived in the United States after 1759. It was Julia's doctoral thesis. (That she had earned two doctorates was a secret that few of even her best friends knew until after her death.)

Fred begged her to let him take it home to read. But now she had the book in her hand, and it did not appear that the request would be answered in the affirmative.

"Stewart, you've read this. Tell her she should let me borrow it," Fred urged.

"No, I haven't read it," came from behind the newspaper.

"You haven't read your own wife's book?" Fred asked, incredulous.

"No," came the reply. "I'm told it is very dull."

We did not need to have the paper lowered to know his eyes were "twinkling blue." And Fred did not find the reading dull.

This generous sharing of their books with others eventually grew into Readers' Service, which today continues to expand under the leadership of Rev. and Mrs. Gwilym Lloyd. Its headquarters is at the corner of Main Street and Crickettown Road, in Stony Point, New York.

Few people know that it began in 1917, in the home of a young bride and groom in Canton, China. Julia and Stewart were concerned that good books were becoming a luxury item in missionary homes, and that Chinese who knew English found little available in that language. The Kunkles not only gave away their own books but also started collecting books from friends in America.

In an article for *Outreach* magazine, a forerunner of *Concern,* Julia wrote:

> How we welcomed the postman on the days when the American mail came in. Even he who lugged the heavy parcels to our door wore a smile. . . . Soon word got around. Such and such a book we had long heard of had arrived. Someone going up coast stopped in to pick up a mystery yarn and a more substantial book to enjoy on deck. A Salvation Army officer, hearing that books were to be had, came, saw, and went away with an armful. Children from the school for foreigners brought back the collection which had adorned the school shelves for the past three months and took away another consignment. . . . Several dozen volumes went to the browsing room of Lingnan University. Friends from Yunnan took up their

winter's supply. An earnest neighbor asked for "something that will strengthen my faith." Another reader wanted a book in English, for she "couldn't understand American books." A painter friend read every book on art; another read all we had on history. Biography, especially the life of Booker T. Washington and of William Lyon Phelps, was enjoyed by our Chinese neighbors.

After forty years of service, the Kunkles retired, returned to America, and urged the then Board of Foreign Missions to support a program for the distribution of books. Readers' Service began in earnest in the basement of Board headquarters at 156 Fifth Avenue in New York City. In 1955, it was moved to Stony Point.

People from all over the United States send their used books (in good condition) to Readers' Service. Jean Lloyd tells us that a recent report shows that 25,885 books were sent to missionaries and national workers in seventy countries. These were people affiliated with over one hundred different denominations and groups, both Catholic and Protestant.

Among the retired missionaries who have served as directors of Readers' Service are Rev. and Mrs. Calvin Hazlett. People here in Stony Point remember Cal as one of those who played an important part in launching our Senior Citizens' Organization.

As Gertrude and Curtis Williams would say, "One thing leads to another."

Cal and Sara Hazlett are now in Westminster Gardens, Duarte, California, that beautiful estate for retired missionaries, ministers, fraternal workers, and commissioned church workers of The United Presbyterian Church in the United States of America. This leads to a story I love to tell.

A Chinese boy by the name of Frank Shu graduated from Yi Wen Commercial School in Cheefoo, Shantung, China. He became a very successful businessman in this country. For twenty-five years, he pondered on how he could best show his appreciation for mission schools and his gratitude for the teaching he had received. He especially wanted to do something for two of his beloved teachers, Mr. William C. Booth and Rev. Henry Birkel.

In answer to my query, Cal Hazlett wrote: "Yes, I know about it. I was working in the Board rooms during furlough in 1949, when Dr. Lloyd Ruland called me into his office so that I could hold in my hand Frank Shu's check for a million dollars for the first buildings of Westminster Gardens."

It is said that this was the largest amount ever given by an individual to the Presbyterian Board of Foreign Missions. It was not given by an American philanthropist, but by a Chinese Christian. And it so happened that when the building was ready, the time had come for Frank Shu's teachers, William C. Booth and Rev. Henry Birkel, to be among its first residents, thus fulfilling their student's wishes.

It is comforting to know that if and when the time comes, we too may be eligible, and having begun our lives together as missionaries in China, find ourselves provided for by a son of China and by the church which he and we served.

SIXTEEN

There are many of us in this part of the country who will remember the winter of '77. Not only were we locked in by heavy snows with drifts so high few could see over them; ice, too, fell in tiny pellets, melted and froze again until the ice chopper could not make a dent in it. It is a winter I would prefer to forget.

For the previous four years, I'd been going through a depressing experience known to most writers as the dry spell. Everything you send out to publishers, except perhaps a poem now and then, comes back with the "encouraging" note to the effect that the material is excellent but it won't sell. New ideas fade like shadows under the cold sky of a rejection slip. You keep saying to yourself: "What's the use of writing if I can't get anything published? If I could only get this book off my hands, I could settle down to doing another—perhaps that children's book or the one about retirement."

"What do you know about retirement?" (That from the gremlin within who had no business being there!) "Neither you nor Fred has actually retired. And besides, September will soon be here and you haven't finished those three talks for the Long Island Presbyterial Retreat."

I went to work on them at once and forgot my frustrations. The retreat proved to be just the lift I needed. It was held in a beautiful old mansion on Long Island Sound, the former summer home of J. P. Morgan, now the convent of the Sisters of St. John the Baptist. We were the first Protestant retreat that the Sisters had invited. We were made to feel as much at home as if we'd been going there all our lives. I don't think there is one of us who does not look forward to returning.

And what a wonderful group of women! Whether it was an hour of prayer in deep silence or an amusing presentation of the past year's accomplishments, there was the warm feeling of the Presence with us.

I loved every one of those women, and how could I help it? They treated me as the celebrity I wish I were. They had a table full of my books which I had the fun of autographing and which actually seemed to be selling! And I had been telling myself that I might never be able to write again; that I was not young anymore and should be grateful for the books already published; that I must be realistic and accept old age as it came.

Now I was being told how one had been helped by a poem when it was needed; how a book had been passed on to a frustrated young mother who loved it and took courage from it.

"Just keep those books coming," they would say.

I went home ready to "lick my weight in wildcats."

And one beautiful morning in early October, it came to me very clearly that there should be no more talking to myself about that book. I was to sit down and write. At first the words felt stiff and awkward. Then, what a relief, what joy to feel ideas flowing through me! By noon, I had a rough outline. And how delighted Fred was when he came home for lunch and heard that I had spent the morning beginning a new book!

The momentum was in full swing when the gremlin came back to remind me that it was November, and the Christmas preparations were far from being finished. The interruption didn't bother me this time because I had something to go back to. In fact, it was a good time to stop. The whole clan, except Tom and his family and Judy and hers, would be arriving for Thanksgiving. If the Christmas gifts were all wrapped, they could be taken home, and it would save mailing nineteen presents. And Judy's four were to be sent to England and should be off before Thanksgiving anyway. Tom's four could wait to be picked up when they came the week after Christmas.

Alas, the gifts for the neighbors didn't get distributed until long into January. I came down with one of the horrendous flus that were going the rounds. Fred was taken with it before I got out of bed. We were both dreadfully ill through Christmas and New Year's. The children offered to come and help, but we couldn't let them because that particular flu was so very contagious.

Meanwhile, the snow and ice continued. Fred was out shoveling in spite of my remonstrances, but that was not unusual. I remonstrated all of every winter. Perhaps I was more insistent this year because neither of us had our strength back and I knew he was out in the cold feeling as bad as I felt. We were both relieved when our nephew, Bob, Jr., came up from New York after the next storm and did the shoveling.

By January 27, I had looked long enough at the unwrapped and undelivered gifts for the neighbors. Long before we had the flu, the children had been asking, "Are you coming to see us this Christmas?" And we had replied, "Of course we are."

We had always given each one of them a small ornament to hang on the tree, and to take to their own homes when they grew up. Now it was long past New Year's.

We stopped at Marie Allison's with a loaf of date-nut bread and had one for the Ehlers across the street from her. Seeing the number of cars in their driveway, I said: "We'd better not stop there now. It looks as if they had company."

"Oh, Myra, haven't you heard?" asked Marie. "Mal died of a heart attack at two thirty this morning."

We were stunned. Dear Malvin Ehler had been our good neighbor for all the years we had been in Stony Point. We went over at once and wept with his dear, sorrowing family.

Two mornings later at quarter of five, Fred woke me up. I was shocked to find him in a cold sweat. "I've got some pain right here," he said, his closed fist over his chest.

"I guess we know what that means," I said. "I'll call the ambulance."

Both of us could not help thinking, Mal, and now . . .?

"Call Dr. Ruthen first," said Fred. "Then call the police and they'll call the ambulance."

Fortunately, I had all three numbers near the phone beside our bed. And before I could throw on some clothes, the police officer was at the door with an oxygen tank. He called the ambulance at once. Fred hadn't needed the oxygen, but how wise to have it so quickly available! I was shocked to hear that there had been so many false alarms for the ambulance that the rule had to be made that a police officer see the patient before calling out the vehicle; frightening when a delay of four to five minutes just might mean death. But our volunteer crew was already at the door, and we were on our way over dangerously icy roads to the hospital in Nyack, some fourteen miles away.

We had faced death together many times in our life —within the sound of gunfire during the Sino-Japanese War, sometimes near enough for the bullets to drop in our yard. We had had to make a dangerous trip across Shantung Province in a truck filled with our family and household goods, across bridges, the floors of which were two planks; below, the raging flood. Always the thought would come: Is this it? Is this the end?

Now his pulse was thready, his face like cold wax. I clung to the verse which had come to me during that brief moment when I was waiting for Dr. Ruthen to come to the phone: "I will not leave thee nor forsake thee."

By the time we got to the emergency room, the pain had become severe and Fred was asking for medication, which he was given at once. I could be most thankful that our small town had equipped its ambulance with a direct line through to the hospital. Everything was ready and waiting—the intravenous solutions, the electrocardiograph, and so forth.

Now I had to leave him to give the nurse the statistics for his chart. It had been a comfort to have my hand on his pulse, to know that that beloved heart was still beating. The Highland fling antics showing up on the monitor were not reassuring. I called our eldest son, Jim, on Long Island. He could get to us quickest and would phone Carl in Boston. It was still early in the morning and we could let the others sleep a while longer. Perhaps the news would be better after I had talked to Dr. Ruthen.

Jim and his wife, Dixie, made record time. How comforting it was to have them near! It turned out that Carl was preaching in Houston, Texas, and would take a plane immediately after the morning service. Soon the children would all know and we would have their love and their prayers to support us.

It was a time of learning: not only how much Fred was loved by everyone, not only how very much we loved each other, but also how very precious life is and how suddenly vulnerable the human body can become. To see that strong, healthy man weakly clinging to those strands of healing was a very different experience from what we had imagined when all was well and we had looked ahead to what *might* happen someday. I think we always pictured it as war or an accident— something that would strike us both at once.

I was now learning how much Fred had been doing for me, how dependent on him I had become: his shopping on the way home from work, his reaching for things on shelves too high for me, his carrying the heavy ironing board I couldn't lift, his moving the guest room bed from the wall and putting it back after I had changed the sheets—all these "little" things which I had so taken for granted. It might be a long time before he could do them again. I smothered the thought that it might be never and went to work.

Jim spent an afternoon teaching me how to get the car in and out of the basement garage without removing the iron support from the living room above.

"You can surprise Dad when he gets home," Jim said. "Remember what he said when you got your driver's license—'Now I can have my coronary in peace'?"

I hadn't remembered it. Strange that when he said it, I had thought of it as a joke.

As soon as Vicki arrived, we went shopping for a lightweight ironing board, some casters for the guest room bed, and a crock pot so that I could make soups for Fred's low-salt diet that would still have flavor.

I gave away the heavy plants that I couldn't lift but had to be moved when we used the tea table. George Lee, his wife, and their daughters would redo the yard in spring so that there would be no heavy gardening.

And I found I *could* "change an electric light bulb," add water to the furnace, clean out a stopped drain, carry out the garbage cans, drive in and out of the dry cleaner's parking lot, and many other things I had feared when I had looked ahead to a possible future alone—things I could help him do now as he was convalescing.

Fortunately, healing was taking place and after three months, he would be back at work in his own hospital.

We owed so much to so many people: to the prayers of friends and strangers; to those dear people of our church who had set up a schedule so that someone was at the door to take me over icy roads to the hospital and back; to the nurses and technicians; to the blessing of a highly qualified doctor. And to the sustaining love and continuing help of our children—those who could come and those who couldn't.

"We didn't have you as an investment," I told them, "but we are certainly reaping dividends, not only now, but we have been all your lives."

And as for that gremlin, he, she, or it could no longer say that I knew nothing about full retirement. For three months, Fred and I enjoyed it. Mornings we work-played. I went back to my writing; Fred sorted and cataloged his stamps and his slides of wild flowers, looked over his Chinese coins, and practiced his recorder music. Then he would settle down to his reading.

I counted the books he had read during his illness—seventeen—which brought the total number since 1943 to 1,068. When he was a child, his mother kept a notebook of the titles and authors of every book she read to him. He has continued the list ever since. Alas, the precious notebook begun by his mother was lost to us during the war with everything else we owned.

Afternoons we went for walks, short ones at first, the distance increasing a bit as time went on. Then I would take him for a drive out into the countryside where we could enjoy the coming of spring, the first buds, the first chipmunk, the first deer.

This year, spring was more than a season, it was a resurrection. The dull bark of the cherry tree just outside our window was now a glistening red, its branches a ballet of blossoms. The lawn, scorched by ice and snow, became green velvet with nosegays of violets. Instead of cold winds rattling the windows, we wakened to birdsong. As soon as we were downstairs each morning, we stepped outside the front door to feel the sponginess and to smell the air—that fresh, delicious air! Earth had never been more beautiful.

These were days when I remembered Fred's mother quoting Browning's lines from "Rabbi Ben Ezra":

> Grow old along with me!
> The best is yet to be . . .

How I had resented the fact that in her old age, she was an invalid, with long months of slow dying in a strange land. "The best is yet to be," indeed!

Now I know that before that, for her and Father Scovel, there had been those beautiful last years alone together. Perhaps it was in memory of those years that she always quoted the rest of the verse also:

The last of life, for which the first was made:
Our times are in his hand
Who saith, "A whole I planned,
Youth shows but half; trust God:
see all, nor be afraid!"

POSTLUDE

Of all the celebrations with which a family is blessed, there is nothing to compare with the Golden Wedding Anniversary:

—not the real wedding, however beautiful, however thrilling, for there are still the tiny ripples of fear of what may lie ahead;

—not the birth of each child, however miraculous that small human being may seem, alive and cuddling in your arms;

—not the many occasions for pride in the children's accomplishments; nor the heartwarming satisfaction of being able to comfort them in disappointment, failure, or sorrow;

—not the delight of their weddings and the deep gratitude to God on seeing that certain radiance surrounding the two who have found each other;

—not the outings, the picnics, the birthdays, the showers of gifts . . . I almost said, not even Christmas, but Christmas is holy and stands alone by itself; but the Golden Wedding Anniversary! It is the culmination, the fulfillment of all a husband and wife have hoped for, dreamed of, and now find to their surprise, has been accomplished!

We celebrated ours early. Judy, John, and their Elizabeth and Joy, ages six and three, were coming from England. Judy hadn't been home in six years, and who knew when she might get home again? So it seemed the best time for our first family reunion since Tom and Janene had left for their mission in Thailand in 1964. I suggested we also make it our Golden Wedding celebration.

"Why not?" said Fred. "We were already in love by then, so there's no need of waiting when it's only a matter of months."

There would be twenty-eight of us: our twelve children (six of ours and the six they brought home to us), plus fourteen grandchildren and the two of us.

What shouts went up as the families arrived at the Scovel-Greeley place in Fitzwilliam, New Hampshire —from Chicago, Pittsburgh, Long Island, Boston, Saranac Lake, Stony Point, and England! Immediately, the girls were squealing and the boys teasing, which again brought us back to their childhood. In no time we were hearing, "Daddy, make Jim stop teasing me," and "Mother, Vicki took my coffee," followed now by hearty laughter instead of whines and tears. It was all such fun.

There was, however, a mood of quiet sadness when Anne announced that their teen-age David couldn't come because of a commitment to his boss. Still, we were proud of his integrity in standing by in the emergency.

Fred and I were waited on from morning till night. I couldn't lift a hand to help with the meals. (I admit I didn't put up much of a struggle.) Everything had been so well planned and carried out so easily and graciously that delicious meals came and went as if the country kitchen had been the Ritz-Carlton.

Gather a few of the Scovel clan anywhere, any evening, and at once, there will be a spontaneous "talent (?) night." It was good to hear again the songs, the conundrums, the puns; to watch the old tricks, all as enjoyable as ever (except for Tom's swallowing fire to the awe and delight of the children and the terror of his mother). This time, it was the grandchildren who stole the show.

Before settling down for the night, we had a prayer and sang a favorite hymn, "Now the Day Is Over."

Fred and I hosted the dinner at the beautiful old Fitzwilliam Inn—all taken care of by Carl and Faith's good friends, the innkeeper Charles Wallace and his wife, Barbara (the well-known singer and soloist at King's Chapel, Boston).

Everything was perfect.

Seeing those beautiful faces gathered around the table was all but overwhelming. Fred felt it, too, and reached for my hand. How could we ever thank God enough for that family! No one could *deserve* all this. Humbling as it could not help being, it was a glorious moment for both of us.

There were walks, and swims, hikes up Mount Monadnock, sings around the piano, all that in the course of our busy lives, we have so little time to do together. It seemed the most natural thing in the world for Carl to gather us in front of the big stone fireplace for a Sunday morning worship service before we went our separate ways—separate, but closer to one another than we had ever been before.

That Sunday morning while Fred and I were having breakfast at the inn, a young waitress for our dinner the night before said, "There seemed to be an awful lot of love in that room."

For all the blessings of this "last of life, for which the first was made," we thank thee, Lord, Amen.

So may it be for you.

ABOUT THE AUTHOR

Myra Scovel, R.N., is the wife of Dr. Frederick Gilman Scovel. They went to China in 1930 as medical missionaries under the Presbyterian Church in the U.S.A. During the Sino-Japanese War, the Scovels lived for six years within the sound of gunfire, once near enough for Dr. Scovel to be wounded seriously. Later, they and their five children were interned by the Japanese in a camp at Weihsien, Shantung. Repatriated on the last trip the *Gripsholm* made from the Orient, the family arrived in New York, December 1, 1943, just in time for Mrs. Scovel to be rushed to the hospital to give birth to their sixth child.

The family returned to China in 1946. After the Communists took over Canton, Dr. and Mrs. Scovel remained at their hospital work for a year and a half, until their position became untenable. In 1953 they were sent to India, where Dr. Scovel became professor of medicine at the Ludhiana Christian Medical College. At his insistence, his wife began work on her first prose book, *The Chinese Ginger Jars,* published by Harper & Row.

Four other books about the family followed, and Friendship Press published five of her juveniles, a teen-age novel, an art poetry book, and three prize-winning plays. The Westminster Press brought out a collection of her poems, *The Weight of a Leaf.*

Myra Scovel is a member of the Poetry Society of America, Women Poets of New York, and the National League of American Pen Women, of which she is a past president of the New York City branch and the present director of its Poetry Workshop.

CHRISTIAN HERALD ASSOCIATION AND ITS MINISTRIES

CHRISTIAN HERALD ASSOCIATION, founded in 1878, publishes The Christian Herald Magazine, one of the leading interdenominational religious monthlies in America. Through its wide circulation, it brings inspiring articles and the latest news of religious developments to many families. From the magazine's pages came the initiative for CHRISTIAN HERALD CHILDREN'S HOME and THE BOWERY MISSION, two individually supported not-for-profit corporations.

CHRISTIAN HERALD CHILDREN'S HOME, established in 1894, is the name for a unique and dynamic ministry to disadvantaged children, offering hope and opportunities which would not otherwise be available for reasons of poverty and neglect. The goal is to develop each child's potential and to demonstrate Christian compassion and understanding to children in need.

Mont Lawn is a permanent camp located in Bushkill, Pennsylvania. It is the focal point of a ministry which provides a healthful "vacation with a purpose" to children who without it would be confined to the streets of the city. Up to 1000 children between the ages of 7 and 11 come to Mont Lawn each year.

Christian Herald Children's Home maintains year-round contact with children by means of an *In-City Youth Ministry*. Central to its philosophy is the belief that only through sustained relationships and demonstrated concern can individual lives be truly enriched. Special emphasis is on individual guidance, spiritual and family counseling and tutoring. This follow-up ministry to inner-city children culminates for many in financial assistance toward higher education and career counseling.

THE BOWERY MISSION, located at 227 Bowery, New York City, has since 1879 been reaching out to the lost men on the Bowery, offering them what could be their last chance to rebuild their lives. Every man is fed, clothed and ministered to. Countless numbers have entered the 90-day residential rehabilitation program at the Bowery Mission. A concentrated ministry of counseling, medical care, nutrition therapy, Bible study and Gospel services awakens a man to spiritual renewal within himself.

These ministries are supported solely by the voluntary contributions of individuals and by legacies and bequests. Contributions are tax deductible. Checks should be made out either to CHRISTIAN HERALD CHILDREN'S HOME or to THE BOWERY MISSION.

Administrative Office: 40 Overlook Drive, Chappaqua, New York 10514
Telephone: (914) 769-9000